FIVE CRIES
OF GRIEF

FIVE CRIES
OF GRIEF

One Family's Journey to Healing

after the Tragic Death of a Son

**Merton P. Strommen
and A. Irene Strommen**

Augsburg
MINNEAPOLIS

FIVE CRIES OF GRIEF
One Family's Journey to Healing after the Tragic Death of a Son

First published 1993 by HarperCollins. Copyright © 1996 Augsburg Fortress Publishers. All rights reserved. Except for brief quotations in critical articles or reviews, no part of this book may be reproduced in any manner without prior written permission from the publisher. Write to: Permissions, Augsburg Fortress, 426 S. Fifth St., Box 1209, Minneapolis, MN 55440.

Scripture is from the Revised Standard Version of the Bible, copyright © 1946, 1952, 1971 by the Division of Christian Education of the National Council of the Churches of Christ in the USA. Used by permission.

Cover photograph by Steven Odland
Cover design by David Meyer

Library of Congress Cataloging-in-Publication Data

Strommen, Merton P.
    Five cries of grief : one family's journey to healing after the
tragic death of a son / Merton P. Strommen & A. Irene Strommen.
        p. cm.
    Previously published: San Francisco, Calif. : HarperSanFrancisco, c1993
    Includes bibliographical references and index.
    ISBN 0-8066-2987-8 (alk. paper)
    1. Bereavement—Religious aspects—Christianity. 2. Strommen, Merton P.
3. Strommen, A. Irene. 4. Strommen, David Huglen, d. 1986. 5. Children—
Death—Religious aspects—Christianity. 6. Strommen family. I. Strommen, A.
Irene. II. Title.
[BV4905.2S787 1996]   96-9285
248.8′6—dc20   CIP

The paper used in this publication meets the minimum requirements of American National Standard for Information Sciences—Permanence of Paper for Printed Library Materials, ANSI Z329.48-1984.   ∞

Manufactured in the U.S.A.   AF 9-2987

00   99   98   2   3   4   5   6   7   8   9   10

To the memory of
David Huglen Strommen

Table of Contents

Acknowledgments

We are grateful to the many readers of our in-process manuscripts and their evaluative comments. A special thanks goes to colleagues at Search Institute—Shelby Andress, Carolyn Eklin, and Dr. Ann Sharma—as well as to our professional friends and associates Dr. Gerald and Marilyn Bolmeier, Dr. William and Lucy Hulme, Dr. Roland and Doris Larson, and Dr. Thomas and Florence Soldahl. Helpful too were our children, whose perceptive reviews were invaluable in shaping our final manuscript: Peter and Normajean, Timothy and Dawn, James and Judy, and John and Heidi.

Thanks too goes to our computer typist, Hertha Lutz, whose interest and attention to detail contributed much.

A special acknowledgment of thanks goes to Roland Seboldt, who initiated the idea of this book, and editor Ron Klug. Ron's careful reading of our manuscript and insightful comments enhanced the book's readability. We appreciate the interest of both men as well as that of the publisher's editorial staff.

Preface

This books tells the story of how we—a mother and father—coped with the tragic death of our twenty-five-year-old son. But we go beyond telling our story to identify what helped us cope with each facet of our grief. We want a grieving person to know the sources of healing that ministered to our needs.

This account of our family's grief journey has several unique features: the way it is organized, its focus on how a mother and a father might grieve differently, its treatment of topics seldom discussed publicly, and its descriptions of how grief affects an entire extended family. Here are some reasons for these unique features.

First of all, we found that the oft-quoted grief stages of Elisabeth Kübler-Ross did not fit our grief journey. True, her conceptual model may describe the stages through which grief progresses in linear fashion for persons coping with a terminal disease. But for us and others whose accounts we have read, the stage theory is misleading. Rather than passing through stages in sequential fashion, we experienced at different times varying intensities of these facets of grief:

> the cry of pain
>
> the cry of longing
>
> the cry for supportive love
>
> the cry for understanding
>
> the cry for significance

For us the *cry of pain* centered in the awareness of a devastating loss that at first caused us to be "bowed in grief." The hurt remains but has now become more like an enveloping mist of sadness that mingles with the joys of life.

The *cry of longing* reflects a pervasive loneliness that comes from missing our son, who remains an integral part of our lives. The cry is an ongoing desire to maintain him in the present tense.

The *cry for supportive love* was more immediate. It arose out of the extreme sense of vulnerability we experienced over our son's sudden death. Emotionally we needed to be embraced in the arms of love, as a sobbing child needs to be held by a parent.

The inevitable "Why?" fuels our *cry for understanding*. It is the effort of our intellect to establish a bridge of understanding between our son's death and our acceptance of it, to attribute meaning to a meaningless loss.

Our *cry for significance* expresses a deep-seated motivation, a compelling drive to see something good come out of seeming tragedy.

These five cries represent recurring facets of our grief.

The pain was overwhelming at first, prompting the cry for supportive love. But in the months that followed, longing and questioning took front stage. Each reappeared in strength at varying times. The quiet resolve to see something meaningful blossom over the grave is always with us.

These five cries, so descriptive of our grief experience, are ones we also hear in the accounts of others who have lost a loved one. A cry voiced by some that we do not treat is the cry of guilt. We leave it out because it was not a factor in our grief experience.

The account you will read is honest. Each of us wrote our descriptions of grief without knowing what the other was including under each cry. Upon reviewing each other's first drafts, we were surprised to find little overlap. The separate accounts that follow show how differently a mother and a father might grieve. This difference may explain in part why tension rises so commonly between grieving parents. Each fails to understand the feelings and reactions of the other.

One feature of this book, and certainly unique to books on grief, is the forthright discussion of dreams, visions, or presence often experienced by grieving persons. Many interpret such events as communication from their departed loved one or as special gifts of comfort from God's spirit. Though they treasure these experiences and speak of them privately to others who grieve, they dare not share them publicly, particularly with a pastor. They often fear that these experiences may be viewed as silly, as aberrations, or as too naive to be taken seriously. So the mysterious events remain hidden from public view.

This book also describes how our son's sudden death affected his brothers, his sisters-in-law, and their children. It is a story they helped us write by sharing memories of the death and their own grief pilgrimage during these past five years. What they shared illustrates further the dynamic nature of grief and its shaping and energizing power.

Does grief over the loss of one's child ever go away? We do not think so. Our experience resembles that of a friend who spoke of grief as a minor chord that throughout one's life will interpenetrate the jubilant major chords of life, giving greater depth to one's love and appreciation of family and friends.

When Lightning Strikes

In a flash the beauty
of your life was seen
Your feet firmly planted
on the earth
Your head and heart
connected to the sky.

—*Tim Strommen*

There was no sense of foreboding for us at 3:30 on that afternoon of August 12, 1986.

Our Buick Le Sabre, with my son Tim's Oldsmobile station wagon close behind, was winding its way down the Arkansas River canyon south of Leadville, Colorado.

I was excited about having completed my first hike above ten thousand feet since my bypass surgery two years before. Together with my husband, Mert; our two oldest sons, Pete and Tim; their wives, Normajean and Dawn; and six grandchildren, we had climbed around Turquoise Lake near Leadville. We were now returning home to our chalet five miles from the town of Buena Vista.

As we broke out of the canyon into the wider expanse of the valley, my thoughts turned to our youngest son, Dave, who was at Frontier Ranch, a Young Life Camp on a slope of Mount Princeton, only eleven miles from our mountain home. I could scarcely wait to tell him about our hike when we would see him the next day. He had expressed concern that he and I might not be able to climb together anymore because of my operation.

Everyone's lighthearted mood was accentuated by the prospect of a two-week vacation together. Only a year before, Tim and his family had returned from living for five years in Dar es Salaam, Tanzania. This vacation would give us all an opportunity for catching up on relationships. The grandchildren were already chattering about the wooden forts they had built and about the possibility of their parents taking them to Breckenridge for the Alpineslide. We adults were talking of tennis, lounging on the deck, hiking, reading, getting in those long conversations we cherish.

Only one son from our family of five would not be present at any time during this vacation. Jim, our third son, with his wife, Judy, and a little daughter, Dana, were home in Minneapolis.

Our fourth son, John, was due to arrive in Denver that very afternoon. After a few days' service project in Denver with his youth group, he, too, would be coming to Frontier Ranch.

Two days earlier we had visited at the ranch with Dave, who had just arrived there with his church youth group from Minneapolis. Last night we had been with him again for a camp rodeo. We saw him relaxed and happy, settling in with his teenagers for a week that he hoped would open spiritual vistas for all of them.

We posed for a picture together, and, before we left, Dave wrote on an envelope the names of his entire group of nineteen and asked us to pray for each person during the coming week. At the end of the list he wrote his own name.

Now, as our two-car caravan approached Buena Vista, the grandchildren reminded Grandpa Mert that he had promised everyone a treat at the Dairy Delite. Soon Mert and I watched fondly as the grandchildren piled out of the two cars, running eagerly toward the drive-in. The children ranged in age from Erik and Alexi at eleven, Andy at ten, Siri at nine, Annelise at seven, to Samuel at six.

Dominating the scene in Buena Vista was Mount Princeton, towering almost directly alongside at fourteen thousand feet. I glanced over at the southeast end of the mountain, where Frontier Ranch lay nestled near the base.

"I hope Dave's had a good day," I said to the others. It looked as though a cloud might have brought a rain shower to the Mount Princeton area.

"Seems as though it always gets cloudy in the afternoon out here," Normajean remarked.

I glanced at my watch and noted that it was about 4:30. Because Mert and I had an errand at the store, everyone else, eager to get back to the chalet, crowded into the station wagon and drove off. When Mert and I approached the driveway of our chalet, we saw our sons Pete and Tim running toward us. Their faces looked gaunt and grim. Tim came up to the window of the car. "There was a message here for us when we came," he said. "Dave's been hit by lightning. He was still alive when the ambulance left for the Buena Vista Clinic."

No time for decisions. No time for deliberating. Mert wheeled the car around. Tim and Pete followed in theirs. The winding five miles down the mountainside seemed forever. I prayed over and over again, "God, keep Dave alive until we come."

At the clinic, Mert and I ran into the waiting room. "No," we were told, "you can't see Dave. The doctors are working on him."

"Is he dying?" I cried. "He's my son—I want to see him!"

"We're sorry," the receptionist said kindly—but firmly. "You'll have to wait here."

Whether it was ten minutes or an hour of waiting, it seemed an eternity.

Then two men approached us and asked us to accompany them. I recognized one as Paul Bruizeman, property superintendent at Frontier Ranch. We followed them down the hall.

I cherished a glimmer of hope. Maybe we were being taken to see Dave. Maybe he had regained consciousness.

The door was opened to an office where two doctors awaited us. Then I knew.

"We've worked on Dave for over an hour," said one of the doctors in a kind, weary voice. "We've done all that could be done. Your son died instantly. The lightning penetrated his mastoid and traveled to his heart, coming out directly below it. At no point during the time we worked on him were we able to establish a connection between heart and brain. At 5:25 we pronounced Dave dead."

"It happened by the ropes course," said the property superintendent, "in the ravine behind the dining hall. Dave's friend Jim Schreyer was with him just before he was struck."

I was overcome by numbness and a sense of unreality. I wanted to see Dave.

The doctor led us into the emergency room.

❧

Mert recalls the scene as though it will always be in the present tense:

"I look at Dave lying on the table, like he is sleeping or has just been running. There is no sign of pain or shock in his face. No sense of evil in the room. But I can tell he is gone—Dave is no longer inside that strong, athletic body of his. His handsome face, skin still alive but purple from the shock of lightning, is frozen in death.

"Unbelieving, we stand around him—we four, with the doctors. I can only say, 'The Lord giveth, the Lord taketh away, blessed be the name of the Lord.' I try to pray, but it is more a prayer of 'Why?' than of resignation. I feel the singed hairs behind Dave's ear, and I stroke his hair. My heart can not believe what my eyes are seeing."

My recollection is in the eternal present, too. I run my fingers through Dave's hair. It is wet. I stroke his face and kiss him on the cheek. I feel the place where the lightning went in behind his ear. I run my hands up and down his limbs.

In one way he looks so natural, as though there had been no pain, no surprise. It is hard to describe, but he even has an eager look, one I have seen many times. I hear Mert saying, "Dave, you went up in a chariot of fire." I keep saying over and over, "I love you, Dave. Thank you, Dave."

But Dave cannot respond. My son is dead.

I see Tim bending over Dave and making the sign of the cross on his forehead.

❧

Outside the clinic, we met Normajean, Dawn, and the grandchildren. Tim walked toward them with both arms outstretched, half-raised, in helpless unbelief.

"He's gone," he said, and then he wept.

The grandchildren watched in silence as Mert broke down in awesome, wrenching sobs. I did not cry much, but I felt a tremendous pain in my chest. It was as though a heavy hand were pushing my head down, and I could not raise it.

We drove back up to the chalet with darkness setting in. The grandchildren ran from the cars and fiercely destroyed all their forts, as if raging against death.

Once in the chalet, Mert asked everyone to gather for prayer. He began to pray but could not finish before he broke down in tears. Eleven-year-old Alexi finished her grandpa's prayer.

Normajean and Dawn set the table and called everyone to eat. The children were crying. Mert kept saying in disbelief, "I am going back to Minneapolis for a funeral." I could not eat. The food was suddenly like ashes in my mouth.

After supper we faced the difficult task of informing the two other brothers of Dave's death. Everyone agreed that John, Dave's soul mate, should not receive the news by phone. Pete and Tim would tell him personally. Immediately they set out for Denver, a trip of 120 miles.

It was left to Mert to call Jim in Minneapolis. I still have a clear image of Mert standing by the phone in the hallway of the chalet, making one of the most dreaded of all calls—a father telling his son that another son is dead.

I heard Mert saying, "Dave was hit by lightning." I knew from the ensuing conversation that Jim did not immediately grasp that it was fatal.

"They couldn't get Dave's heart started, Jim," Mert said. "Dave is gone."

Only later did we learn that this day had not been an easy one for Jim. His wife, Judy, four months pregnant, had been bleeding. Because there was real danger of a miscarriage, she was to see the doctor the next morning. If she were to miscarry, it would be the second time they had lost a child. All of us knew how much they looked forward to having another baby.

Normajean, Pete's wife, succeeded in getting the children, who were crying hysterically, to create in art forms what they were feeling.

Sometime in the early evening there was a knock on the door. It was the pastor from the church we had attended the previous Sunday. His visit brought the dimension of faith to a numb, bewildered, hurting family.

Other tasks emerged. Mert had to go to the mortuary in town. Dawn, Tim's wife, stepped forward. "I'll go with you, Mert," she said. It was comforting for me to see Mert being helped by a daughter-in-law, he who had no daughters of his own.

Soon after midnight, Pete and Tim returned from Denver, bringing John with them.

My heart ached for John. One look at his face, one feel of his body as we embraced each other, and I knew he was frozen, numb, disbelieving. He desperately wanted to *see* Dave, but he could not, not until several days later at the reviewal in Minneapolis.

We learned then the poignant drama connected with John's finding out about Dave. A few minutes before Pete and Tim arrived, John had called Jim, asking him to buy plane tickets to New York for himself and Dave. They had planned a trip there for the next week but had forgotten to secure their tickets. Jim, knowing his brothers were already on their way to bring the tragic news, hesitated to tell a puzzled John why he could not buy those tickets. Finally, he had to tell John that Dave was dead. Fortunately, Pete and Tim arrived just as John was putting down the receiver following this painful conversation.

ॐ

Shortly after the three brothers returned to the chalet from Denver, Jim Schreyer, Dave's very close friend and fellow counselor from Bayport, drove over from Frontier Ranch. There, in the chalet, in the early hours after midnight, Schreyer described the events surrounding Dave's death.

The day had been beautiful at Frontier Ranch, as it had been for us on our hike above Turquoise Lake, but in the afternoon, clouds had begun to accumulate. Soon there was a rain shower with the promise of more to come.

For an hour or so after the noon meal, Dave had been outside the dorm talking with a counselor from Bayport. Around a quarter to four, Schreyer came by to say that some of the Bayport group were inquiring about chances to go on the ropes course. Their time as a group had been scheduled for 4:00. Some of the group doubted that they could go because of the rain, but Dave had offered to check it out.

At about ten minutes to four, Dave had taken off at a jogging gait for the ravine where the ropes course was located. As Schreyer explained it, that meant crossing over a bridge and then continuing on a path high along the side of a ravine. After a short distance, steps cut off sharply from the path and descended to the ropes course.

Schreyer said that almost right after Dave had left, one of the Bayport campers came running into the lounge with the report of a blinding flash of lightning. The others had not seen it because the lounge was so far back in the building, but all heard the deafening clap of thunder, which frightened campers and horses alike.

"Did you make any connection between Dave and the lightning?" Pete asked.

"Not really," Schreyer said. "A quick, heavy shower followed the thunderclap, but I guess I only wondered where Dave found shelter."

"When did you realize that something had happened?" John asked.

"Maybe five or ten minutes later, when Dave didn't come back. I went out into the court, where some Bayport kids were waiting for Dave to play Ping-Pong with them.

"I saw people running back and forth in a confused way. I heard that someone had fallen off the ledge and into the ravine."

We all were silent, picturing the scene.

"Reports started to come that someone from Minnesota was hurt. A man came up to me and asked if I was from Minnesota." Schreyer stopped talking and choked back the tears. "I was afraid to ask why, but then I did. He told me that Dave had been struck by lightning.

"I tried to get over by the ropes, but they wouldn't let me. I went back to the Bayport kids. But then I couldn't stand it. I tried a second time, and they let me through."

There was silence again. We were all crying.

Schreyer continued. "I went over to the path. About four steps below me, I saw Dave's body. Just then two doctors came by me and went down to him. There was a nurse with them. Several people were already there giving CPR. I recognized some of the camp counselors.

"It was awful." Jim was sobbing now. "I wanted to run down. I wanted to yell, 'Dave, get up! Get up!' But it was like I was paralyzed. I couldn't move. I saw his face. I *knew* he was dead."

John got up and walked over to Jim and put his arms around him.

Agonizing as it was to hear Schreyer's words, it was a relief to know the details of Dave's death.

We remained silent for a while—each in our own tears—our own pain.

Before Schreyer left to go back to Frontier Ranch, he asked if he could read Psalm 139, which he said Dave had been memorizing:

> Whither shall I go from thy Spirit?
> Or whither shall I flee from thy presence?
> If I ascend to heaven, thou art there!
> If I make my bed in Sheol, thou art there!
> If I take the wings of the morning
> and dwell in the uttermost parts of the sea,
> even there thy hand shall lead me,
> and thy right hand shall hold me,
> If I say, "Let only darkness cover me,
> and the light about me be night,"
> even the darkness is not dark to thee,
> the night is bright as the day;
> for darkness is as light with thee.

Black darkness, even though God was in it, characterized that sleepless night—in the chalet, at Jim and Judy's house, and everywhere the word had gone to those who loved Dave.

ধ্ৰ

August 13 was a clear, beautiful day in the mountains. As the cars moved down the mountainside, away from the Strommen chalet, none looked back. I privately wondered if I could ever return. Dawn and Tim took Mert and me to the airport. The rest would follow in cars and arrive home a day later.

At the Minneapolis airport we were met by Jim, Judy, and their two-year-old daughter, Dana; Mert's brother, Luther, and his wife, Helen.

Once home, the series of "firsts" began for us; most painful of all was entering the house Dave had left so recently. I cried and hugged his picture. Then I turned to our daughter-in-law, Judy, patted her gently on the stomach, and said, "But we have a new little life coming."

Judy began to cry. Then Mert and I knew that death had come twice to the Strommen family.

1   The Cry of Pain

My tears are the words with which I tell God of my pain.
—*Adolfo Quezada*

A Mother's Cry

Born of a mother's pain
You were her fifth boy
From her you learned of love
From you she learned of joy.
—*Tim Strommen, unpublished song*

No matter how many ways I have tried to describe my pain through these years—in journal and in conversation—it always takes a form of the same thought: something has been wrenched, ripped, torn out of me.

I am an earthly mother. My cry is a Mother Cry, universal and yet fiercely individual. So I share my cry with others of you who have lost a child. None of us mourns exactly like any other. But we are a vast sisterhood down through the centuries, bonded by pain and joy—felt and expressed—in a thousand ways.

The thought of Mary the mother of Christ has come into my mind many times. The prophet Simeon said to her in the temple, "A sword will pierce through your soul."[1] As a mother who has lost her son, I have felt that sword many times. I understand, too, how utterly helpless Mary must have felt as she stood by the cross, unable to understand, able only to love and hurt.

Unable to understand, able only to love and hurt. That is my cry of pain.

Love, hurt, wonder. These elements were in my cry of pain when Dave was born. I hurt fiercely, physically, at the moment of his birth. But I also felt warm, overflowing love when I saw my fifth son for the first time. Wonder at the miracle of birth was stronger than my understanding of it at that moment.

During the twenty-five years of Dave's life, there were times when I was especially conscious of my oneness with him, times when he was ill or troubled. Deep within my heart there was always the knowledge of a vast reservoir of love and identification. I believe this is part of being a mother.

Three days before the fatal lightning strike, as I had waited for Dave to arrive safely from Bayport, Minnesota, with his youth group, I knew that my yearning to see him was unusually intense. The same feeling was present the next day at Frontier Ranch when I wanted to talk to him—alone—and could not. It was like a frustrating dream in which, even though the person you love is near, you cannot reach him.

In some inexplicable way I believe the unborn sense that I must say good-bye to a part of myself was emerging closer to my conscious mind. The instant we heard on Tuesday, "Dave has been struck by lightning," the process of parting was set in motion.

As we waited in the Buena Vista Clinic on that afternoon of August 12, I became aware of pains deep within me, mounting in intensity. In wonder, I recognized them as the hard bearing-down pains of child labor, the final push before birth. I do not remember having any fear, only the ability to identify the pains. Before we were called into the doctor's office, the pains had gone as mysteriously as they had come.

A week or so later we received a letter from Laura, a friend of our daughter-in-law Normajean. She wrote:

> We have wept with you as fellow parents, of feeling the anguish and pain of losing a part of you. The intensity of joy at receiving an infant from the hand of our gifting God must be similar to—almost the antithesis of—the unbearable pain of having to return him—prematurely from our perspective—to the giver and receiver of life!

This young woman touched the heartbeat of what happened when I lost my son Dave. I felt in my body the pain of losing a part of me.

When we were ushered into the emergency room at the clinic and I first saw Dave's lifeless body, I remember doing something that even at the time seemed instinctive. I ran my hands up and down his body, especially his limbs, to the tips of his toes. I could not have said why I did that, but it felt right.

Four years later, at the Passion Play in Oberammergau, I experienced a flashback of that emergency room scene when I saw Mary handling Jesus' body after it was taken down from the cross. One of her first actions was to run her hands up and down each of her son's limbs. When I remarked about this to my friend Beulah, who also attended the performance, she became very thoughtful and said, "I noticed that, too. I did that when my little boy died when he was seven years old. That was twenty years ago, and I still remember doing that."

I wonder if it is one of the acts of parting for a mother.

As we left the emergency room and walked outside the clinic, in all the confusion of crying grandchildren, I remember saying, in desolation of spirit, "There will never be an ordination. There will never be a *kransekake.*"

I think this simple cry carried a heavy weight. In it were the seeds of the pain I was to carry in my heart after Dave's death.

It was the cry of unfulfilled dreams, of incompleteness. Dave would never fulfill his dream of entering the ministry. Ordination, to me, was the symbol of that decision. But there would be none. And the *kransekake.* In Scandinavian tradition this is a series of almond rings proudly pyramiding to the top to form a celebrative cake. It is a symbol of festivity, of honor. Pete, Tim, and Jim had already each had his *kransekake.* John's day would come. I was looking forward to making it for Dave at his ordination. Now I was hurting because part of my mother joy had been taken from me. I was hurting because our family would never be complete again.

Pain of Body and Spirit

The pain of loss to both spirit and body showed itself in many ways during those first hours after Dave's death. Back at the chalet, around 9:00 that evening I suddenly felt with a terrible, frightening certainty that I was going to be very sick. I began to tremble; waves of nausea swept over me.

I took refuge in the bedroom. The darkness in that room was dense, the blackness heavy. *I am falling apart!* I cried in desperation. *What shall I do?*

Then something happened for me. I thought of my cardiac rehabilitation classes at the hospital back in Minneapolis. Ever since my open-heart surgery two years before, I had gone regularly to these sessions. There we learned the importance of reading our bodies.

I *will not fall apart,* I said to myself.

I took my pulse. Nothing was wrong there.

I lay down on the bed and began my deep, even breathing. Over and over. Over and over. Deep and even. Deep and even.

What if I have to do this all night? I asked myself. *That's all right, too,* I answered. *I'll keep on if I have to do this until I die.*

Deep and even. In and out. Somewhere along the way I felt my body was relaxing. I was lying quietly; the trembling was gone. My stomach churning had stopped.

The pain of the spirit was not gone. There had been a profound assault on my inner self, one the effects of which I would feel for a long time. The knife was still turning; there were still tears. But as my son John told me when he heard about it, "That night there was a kind of rebirth beginning for you, too, Mother."

I like to think so. Along with the calming of my body, a glimmer of light came into my spirit. It was as though this was God's sign to me: "You can cope, Irene. You will make it. I am with you."

Coping with the Cry of Pain

The pain of the initial hours described here was only the beginning of my grief experience. Although pain of spirit is predominant in facing loss, I was also conscious of times when the pain seemed physical. I often described it as a knife turning in my chest. Through the ensuing years since Dave's death I have learned again and again how intricately pain of body and pain of spirit are interwoven.

When the realization sank in that Dave was really gone, I sensed that I had been suddenly impelled into the center of a storm. The image I saw was of myself as a young girl walking to school in the prairie town of Govan, Saskatchewan, on a wild January day. The wind was blowing stinging pellets of snow against my face, and I could see myself thrusting my head down and forward into the teeth of the gale. I knew that would be the only way to get to my destination.

Very soon after Dave's death, I determined that I would not try to go around the storm of grief. I would lean into it and go through.

There may be a long road ahead of me yet, but I believe the intentionality of my decision was significant. What has helped me through the storm?

Having Respect for My Body

I believe my body is my friend and will fight for me if I allow it to do so. Consequently, I have tried to maintain good sleep habits, eat nutritionally, and be regular in my exercise program. During the first months after Dave's death, my son Pete and I took long brisk "talking" walks together, accomplishing two constructive things at once. Exercise has always been important in our family. Sons Jim, Tim, and John and daughter-in-law Judy spoke often of the healing value of running in the first years of their grief.

Talking to Myself and God

I have often talked aloud to God about my pain, my doubts, my fears. Driving alone in the car has been a great place for doing that. Doing it while exercising is another.

Pete worked through his own grief by walking long distances each day on a path through the rocky terrain above Lake Superior.

These were times of giving vent to his emotions by crying and talking to God. Often he talked to Dave as he walked. These long walks were powerfully therapeutic, he feels. In the process, he realized there were two levels of grief for him, one for the brother now his peer, and one for the little baby fourteen years younger than him. In his teen years, Pete had been a responsible caregiver for his baby brother Dave.

Talking with Others

There have been the more formal times of making presentations on grief in church worship settings or participating in small-group discussions. Easily the most frequent and ongoing have been conversations with family and friends, as well as others who have lost a child or a sister or a brother. We have shared our pain and learned from each other. Interesting things have happened in our exchange. I have clarified my own thinking and gained insights. I have also learned that there can be some remarkable similarities between grief feelings of parents and siblings.

Sometimes I have been helped to name my own pain by hearing others name theirs. Recently I was in conversation with my friend Tom about the loss of his brother, with whom he had been very close in age and spirit. That also had been a sudden and catastrophic death. Now twenty years in the past, Tom still reflects with emotion, "When I lost my brother, it was kind of like the end of my age of idealism. I had to grow up. I had to find out who I was." When our son John heard this, he identified immediately. "That's exactly what it has been for me," he said.

On another occasion, Tom, who has had his own bouts with illness, said this: "Sometimes I think it wouldn't be bad to die quickly. Then I could see my brother again." The anticipation and longing shone in his eyes as he said those words.

I was immediately reminded of John's words to me one day: "You're lucky, Mom. You'll see Dave much sooner than I will." Most likely I will, but knowing this is not a depressing feeling. When I had my bypass surgery, for some reason the first sustained image I had when I came out of anesthesia was Dave's face coming toward me in a mist. I think now that is what I will see when I die.

Using Creative Forms to Express Grief

To express my emotions, I chose a method that made use of my interests. Journaling regularly brought release of spirit and rich fulfillment as well as a chance to learn more about my reactions to life's stress and pain and how I could combat them.

Facing Painful Situations Related to My Grief

Of course, the place that symbolized the greatest pain of all was the site of Dave's death in Colorado. The next summer, Mert and I went for the first time to see the site of Dave's death. Lisa, the nurse who had given him CPR, accompanied us.

I found the place rather awesome, with its steep sides forming almost a vee-shaped bottom in which there was a rushing stream. Tall trees. Earthen steps wide apart, steps that went down sharply to the tree where the ropes course began.

"This is the step," said Lisa, pointing to the third one from the bottom. I knelt on the ground and kissed the place where he had fallen.

Brother Tim suggested we have a memorial observance each year out in Buena Vista. He told us that among the Indian members of his church in Dar es Salaam this was a custom, and he felt it would be a meaningful one for us, too.

All four brothers returned to our chalet in the mountains for the first anniversary of Dave's death. As I waited for their cars to arrive for our memorial observance, I went out for a walk on the road above the chalet. I was crying. What a miserable experience this was going to be! The brothers did not need to see their mother crying. I should be happy to see them, but I could not be happy.

Gradually I became aware of Dave's presence. I heard his voice, how or where I do not know. It was comfortable and low-key, just like always.

"Now you're feeling sorry for yourself, Mom," he said.

I answered aloud, "I am, aren't I?"

The answer came back. "Yes, you are, Mom."

I turned around and walked back to the chalet.

God, give me courage to accept the things I cannot change, I prayed, and God allowed me to greet everyone a few minutes later with glad, open arms.

August 12, 1987, was a beautiful day. In the morning the whole family drove up to Cottonwood Pass and had lunch by the little mountain tarn where Dave, John, and their dog Pal had romped many times. It was a scene that brought back poignant family memories. It is for us one of the loveliest of the high places.

Then we drove back to Frontier Ranch. We paused outside the dorm and tried to imagine Dave as he left his youth group and began jogging to the bridge that would then lead to the path above the ravine. It was strange to walk that path, the last one Dave ever walked on this earth. Each, from the youngest to the oldest, was engrossed in private thought. I wondered what Dave was thinking about in those last moments of life.

We came to the place where the steps descend sharply to the ropes course. We walked down to the third step from the bottom. *Did he pause right before it happened? Did he sense anything strange? Was he just turning his head to begin the run back when lightning struck?*

Three-year-old Dana expressed it for all of us: "I feel very sad," she said.

Back at the chalet we had our memorial service. We knew it meant a step toward healing, but it was hard because Dave was still intensely ours.

Two days later, I awoke in early morning and began to think of the painful pull between the past and the present. Yet, what would happen if the hurt went away? Would the memories fade?

A "word" came to me that morning. This is what I heard in my mind: "I will take the hurt away, but the love will not be taken away." It fell on me like a benediction. I went back to sleep.

I am no longer afraid that I might forget, that memories might fade. There is a space within me that will always be for Dave.

Each year on the twelfth Mert and I have a memorial service at the chalet. Most of the brothers and their families have been able to join us at one time or another. The services have been poignant, tender times of remembering Dave and thanking God for his presence with us.

Facing the hard place has helped the sharp edges of pain to soften. This year, when we stood at the site of Dave's death, I heard my brother, who was standing beside me, say, "This is where Dave met God." My sister said, "I feel as though it is holy ground." A sense of peace came into my being when I realized that I could say those things, too.

A Father's Cry

Seared on my mind is a scene that replays itself like a videotape. I see Tim and Pete bursting out of the chalet, running down the steps toward my car with drawn, grim expressions on their faces. Their first words continue to reverberate in my mind like an echo bouncing off the walls of a canyon: "Dave has been hit by lightning, but he's still alive."

"Still alive"—these chilling words spoke to the seriousness of the strike. Vaguely I heard the rest: "He's at the clinic where they have taken him in an ambulance."

Soon I saw his strong, athletic body lying motionless on a table, void of the spirit that made him Dave. My youngest son—my piano player, choir director, youth counselor, future pastor.

I was totally unprepared for the pain that broke upon me. Until then I had been spared the experience of tragic grief. I was a person unacquainted with bitter loss.

Years ago, realizing how little I knew about grief, I interviewed a friend who had just lost his young wife. My notes of his experience went into a box to review before writing letters of condolence. I was, to use the words of a good friend and seminary president, Dr. Alvin Rogness, "among the elite with respect to suffering." He used these words about himself because he, too, had been a novice with respect to grief until he lost his son Paul, age twenty-four.

Bent Low in Grief

As I stood outside the clinic, my numbness broke, and my whole being reacted to the loss of my son. Sobs began deep in my inmost being and moved up my body, contorting it forward. Never before had I understood what it meant to be "bent low in grief." It bent my body forward and my head down.

I, who rarely shed tears, cried out in pain. I, who had learned as a research scientist to be objective about life's problems, was now suddenly catapulted into an experience I had never known. I had lost someone I loved deeply; something had been torn out of my body; part of my future had been wrested away.

One might counter, "But you still had four loving sons, three lovely daughters-in-law (Heidi, the fourth one, came two and a half years later), a wonderful life companion, and seven grandchildren. Didn't this wealth make it easier for you to lose a son?" No, it did not.

Like the roots of a tree, my love for Dave—like my love for his brothers, their wives, and their children—had penetrated into the depths of my being. Tearing out this root from my life created a black hole in my inner being. I came to realize that the deeper one's love for a son, the more devastating the grief.

The time when the pain of losing my son was most unbearable was the day Irene and I entered the Morris Nilsen Funeral Home to pick out a casket. For that I needed the support of my brother. Walking up and down the aisles, I saw caskets designed for elderly people; I was there to choose one for my youngest son. The pain of loss was overwhelming.

Thankfully, Morris Nilsen at an earlier time had ordered a casket covered with blue denim. He was not surprised when we chose that one for Dave.

Then I had to pick out a gravesite—and I had still not chosen a gravesite for myself or Irene. The strangeness of driving to a plot of ground among the green shrubbed hills of Lakewood Cemetery gave way to an awful reality. The soil and grass being pointed out by the salesman were to cover our youngest son. The fragility of life broke upon me with a new awareness. The gravesite became a sharp reminder of the imminence of my own final day.

Later, we as a family surrounded Dave's casket before the public reviewal. Jim and John, who had not seen his body in death before, lovingly, with tears, moved their fingers over Dave's cold, waxlike body. I experienced the truth that pain is the price we pay for being alive, that vulnerability to death is one of the given conditions of life.[2]

An especially tender time for me occurred when I was with my grandchildren. They, who many times had wrestled with Uncle Dave on the floor and laughed at his zany jokes, had decided to put roses on his casket. I took them to Bachman's, a florist in Richfield, to purchase the flowers they were going to buy with their own money. When they saw the not-yet-unfurled roses, they quickly turned to a display of colorful carnations. I listened to them deliberate as each chose a different color, debating which should be for each. As I heard them talk about their Uncle Dave and the flowers they were going to give him, my heart broke. I turned aside quickly to a side aisle so that my tears could remain private.

Losing a Child

In the months that followed, I was surprised to have several people who had lost a spouse, parent, and child tell me, "The grief I experienced over losing my child was more intense even than that of losing my spouse or parent."

Not until I had lost Dave did I realize how profoundly and inextricably his life was linked with mine. How deeply I loved him.

Intensifying my sense of loss were hundreds of tender memories.

I would remember fun times when we as a family were sitting around the dinner table. When it came time for free prayers, Dave as a little boy would go on and on with his prayer. His brothers, eager to be finished with evening devotions, would start saying, "Amen, amen," until Dave obligingly stopped.

I would think of Dave befriending the lonely and alienated. As a teenager trained in Peer Ministry (a training program in friendship skills), Dave had reached out to a classmate who had been shunted from one foster home to another. Dave's reaching out had changed his friend's life, forming a friendship that lasted until Dave's death.

I would see Dave singing in *The Fantasticks* at Richfield High School or playing basketball with his brothers in our driveway. I would think of how he gave two weeks of his vacation to paint his brother's house when Pete was down in bed with back trouble. Every treasured memory formed an emotional tie that continues to bind me to Dave.

Losing Part of Myself

I have lost more than a son I admired. I have also lost part of myself, because part of myself resides in each of my sons. Each one has qualities, talents, and interests I treasure for myself.

I love to play the piano. Of our five sons, Dave was the piano player. After his death we noted the scratches his fingernails had made on the board above the keys. Not until five years later did we have the heart to refinish this portion of our Steinway. The day I was able again to play the piano, tears flowed. Then I realized how much our lives were tied together in piano playing.

My professional training is in psychological counseling. Once, when training youth leaders in how to use a counseling profile, I noticed how Dave excelled as a counselor and told him so. He could enter into the feelings and life perspective of another person in a remarkable way. He responded to people in ways I had been trying to cultivate.

At one time I considered making choir directing a life vocation. At age fifteen I was already directing a church choir and male chorus. Dave inherited that talent. Though he had never seen me direct, he used the same motions I did and interpreted choir anthems as I would. When I watched him direct a choir, it was like seeing myself. Now that part of my life is gone.

Losing part of myself includes losing part of my future—the future that will never be. This painful realization came to Irene and me as we watched the seminary graduating class march down the aisle of Central Lutheran Church. Dave should have been with that robed class, looking forward to his first call as youth pastor.

I felt the loss of my dreams for Dave's future that joyous evening when John married Heidi. Standing with John in that cathedral-like church of Central Lutheran were four groomsmen, his three brothers and his friend Steve, who stood in Dave's place.

Gone was the possibility of Dave being married and having a family. Gone was the possibility of visiting his home, hearing about his work, playing with his children.

The cry of pain. What are its facets? According to the much-quoted stage theory of Kübler-Ross, anger is one. The assumption is that if we lose something we prize dearly, our natural reaction is anger.

Reaction to Pain

When Dave's cousin John Christopherson, then completing his doctorate at the University of Chicago, heard the news, he reacted with anger: "How tragic! Senseless! When I think of other young men who live in my Chicago neighborhood—who have robbed our next-door neighbors at gunpoint, stolen friends' cars, raped a classmate—I become very angry. God, where are you? Don't you care? David's life, given to harmony, has been stopped by a freakish accident, while others prosper in their works of dissonance and destruction. Why, God? Why?!"

This was also the response of our grandchildren. Upon hearing that their uncle had been hit by lightning, the six grandchildren (ages six to eleven) reacted in rage. They rushed outside and began to demolish the "forts" they had carefully constructed out of dead branches and pieces of wood.

In the midst of my cry of pain, I felt no anger. In my mind, no one was to blame for Dave's death except lightning, which strikes the earth hundreds of thousands of times each year. I did not blame God for the lightning or for allowing Dave to be at the fatal spot when the lightning exploded. I have spent no time rehearsing the idea that if he had walked instead of jogged to the ropes course, he might still be living.

I suppose my worldview, an important factor in coping with grief, altered what might be termed normal reactions. When Dave was baptized, Irene and I gave him back to God. That placing of our son in the arms and care of God may have caused me to say at the clinic, "God has taken him up in a chariot of fire." I saw a loving God using the occasion of his death to move Dave to another arena of activity. The only anger or irritation I have known against God has occurred during an occasional period of prayer. At such times my exchanges with God have been heated and sharp. My protest was not the loss of Dave but rather the invisible wall separating me from him. Because of my strong desire to communicate with Dave, I felt that the phrase "communion of saints" in the Apostles' Creed was not being realized. I was irritated, rightly or wrongly, that some form of communion was being denied me, and I told God so. My protests did not change God, but the release of feeling brought things back into perspective for me.

An illustration of my sensitivity of spirit came in an incident that intensified my pain. While at Frontier Ranch, Dave had been taking pictures on his 35mm camera. Several times he had asked friends to take closeups of him. For that reason I prized the exposed film I found in his camera. I felt that the chance to see these closeups would be like seeing him again.

I waited eagerly for the company to process the film and send back the slides. They never came. Of the hundreds of thousands of rolls of film the company processes, this one was sent to the wrong place and could not be traced. It was lost.

Taking It like a Man

In our society strength is often associated with suppressing grief. The man who shows no tears during a tragedy is often described as "taking it like a man." A bereaved husband is often asked, "How's your wife doing?" by others who assume the husband is less affected by grief. We in America assume the grieving process should be private and brief, in contrast to the highly ritualized mourning practices in other cultures. We believe that within three months a person's grief should be ended, and certainly within a year. In contrast to this expectation, studies show that many bereaved people suffer an average of twenty years following the death of a loved one.

Suppressing grief, as our culture encourages, only buries the emotion alive. When forced underground, grief can have destructive effects, both physically and psychologically. However, if expressed fully, grief can be an occasion for growth and new creativity.

I was aware from research reports I had read that people who have lost a loved one are at risk for at least a year following the death. The stress of grief can lead to cancer, infectious diseases, cardiovascular disorders, damaging behavioral changes, depression, sleep disorders, or loss of interest in life.[3] It can also have a devastating effect on a marriage. Several studies have shown that most parents who have lost a child through cancer are involved in serious discord or divorce within a year.[4]

I took these reports seriously, recognizing that unexpressed grief could make us vulnerable to later illness. Therefore, Irene and I made a conscious decision to face our grief the way one walks into the full fury of a storm. It was a decision we reaffirmed weeks later while on a vacation trip that brought us to lovely Camden, Maine, with its harbor of white sailing vessels bobbing in the sun. While walking down a road leading to the harbor, we were talking about Dave and how we would continue to treat our grief. We decided against asking God to heal the wound or remove the pain created by Dave's death, because that would suggest allowing Dave to recede in our memory. Believing that God transferred him for another purpose—a higher calling—we decided also to cultivate an active sense of his living on the other side of an invisible wall "in an adjoining room." We were determined to maintain Dave in the present tense as one who continues to work with us in carrying out God's mission.

Facing Painful Reminders

In retrospect, I believe I was helped most by our decision not to shrink from grief-stimulating situations. Experiences I thought would be unbearable actually reduced the pain. I am referring to such traditional practices as a public reviewal with an open casket, a funeral in the church where one's child grew up, and a committal service beside an open grave. Each ritual is based on a traditional wisdom that death needs to be faced openly.

Rather than considering pictures of Dave to be painful reminders of loss, we hung enlarged photos of him in both our city and mountain homes. I found a company that could take our 1985 family Christmas portrait, isolate the back row picturing the five brothers, and blow up this portion of the portrait to twelve times its original size. This picture of Dave with his four brothers is now affixed to the wall above our kitchen bay window to greet all who enter our house. For my office I had a friend create a large oil painting of Dave sitting on top of Mount Princeton, the mountain where he was killed. This painting was based on a picture of the two of us seated on a rocky perch at the top of this peak, fourteen thousand feet high.

I recognize that some grieving persons cannot tolerate pictures and conversation of their loved one. This was true of an acquaintance of ours, a Chinese waiter. One day when serving us food, he told us his mother had died. Torn with grief, he added this cryptic statement: "I feel like taking my life." Concerned, we tried to stay in touch with him. On the day of his mother's funeral I brought a plant and card to express our condolence. Later that day he called my home and asked if I would take them back. He wanted nothing in his home to remind him of his mother's death following her funeral. His action poses an extreme example of how some fend off painful emotions by forbidding references to or reminders of a loved one's death. But, as Judy Tatelbaum has written, "Grief unexpressed is like a powder keg waiting to be ignited."[5]

A Man in Grief

What helped me most in grappling with the cry of pain?

Accounts of Other Men

I found it helpful to read the moving accounts of others who had lost a young adult son (Adolfo Quezada, Nicholas Wolterstorff, Leighton Ford, Leroy Rouner). Their open expression of grief, their lament of "dreams forever unfulfilled," their insistence on the particularity of grief were reassuring to me. I especially appreciated Quezada's interpretation of the beatitude: "Blessed are they who mourn, for they shall be comforted."[6]

Through his experience of grief he came to see that "if I mourn, if I allow myself to let go and experience all that comes of grief, then and only then, will I find the comfort of new life."[7]

Letters to Dave

Also helpful in coping with my sense of loss was writing letters to Dave in my journal. Here I could converse with him, share my pain, and tell him how much I loved him.

Since then I have discovered that many grieving people write letters like this as a form of therapy. Leighton Ford describes it as a way by which he was able to bring to a close his relationship to Sandy, the son he lost.[8]

Writing letters to a loved one is a powerful tool. It was used at Dave's funeral by those who had unfinished business to settle or final words of endearment to give him. At the suggestion of the funeral director, several people wrote letters to Dave and slipped them into his coffin before the lid was closed. With these letters went love notes and colored pictures from our grandchildren. For those who wrote, it was an important step in alleviating the pain.

Expressing My Grief

Allowing grief to be expressed meant that it sometimes erupted at unexpected times. I was at a Christmas concert of the Dale Warland Singers, thoroughly enjoying the sheer beauty of their choral music, when unexpectedly, the tender Christmas carol "Away in a Manger" evoked memories that caused sobs to convulse my body. All I could do was wait for the pain to subside as tears flowed, hoping no one would notice but those on either side of me.

I had a number of speaking engagements following Dave's death. Fearing that something might trigger an unexpected grief reaction and embarrass the audience, I usually began my speech by telling about my loss. People often thanked me for having opened myself to them and shared my grief experience. I heard, "We came to know you in a new way and feel closer to you as a result." It helped me to share the account of my grief.

Two of our sons followed the same route. Pete, a pastor in Duluth, Minnesota, told his congregation right after the funeral that he had a deep need to talk about the event and did so both in private conversations and in sermons. This openness encouraged church members to talk with him not only about his grief but also about their own.

Daughter-in-law Normajean focused her grief on creative efforts, using calligraphy and dried flowers from Dave's funeral to create framed presentations of Psalm 139. They were gifts to members of the family for their first Christmas. This creative bent found further expression in the beginning of a venture of printing religious greeting cards. Most significantly, Normajean focused her graduate studies in grief counseling and became a grief counselor for a local funeral home.

Tim, also a pastor, told his congregation in Waukegan, Illinois, that he wanted to talk about Dave and invited people to ask about him. This gave permission to people who needed it and opened the door of opportunity for talking with people. It also freed Tim to speak about his grief in sermons.

Several times Irene and I were asked to give a public account of our grief pilgrimage. As we spoke, we could see tears appear as people relived their own (often buried) grief.

After Dave's funeral, a woman told us that her husband had wept through the entire service. He realized later, he told his wife, that he had been weeping for a brother very close to him who had died twenty-five years earlier.

Jim's need to do something about his grief over Dave's death became real the night he was at the hospital with his wife, Judy. Here they lost their little child, who was in the fourth month of gestation. It was a time of struggle and pain. During that night vigil his grief found expression in a poem he wrote entitled "Brother Dave." In this poem he reflects on the short life of his brother, whom "I really saw as a hard worker who didn't come by things easily, but who had a goal and kept pressing toward it." This poem, the first one he had ever written, expresses who Dave was. More than that, it also expresses Jim's belief that he will see Dave again. That conviction came so strongly to Jim in those first agonizing days that he calls this poem his great affirmation.

Brother Dave

Brother Dave, you were just beginning,
Just beginning, yet loved by so many;
Loved by so many yet too humble to realize;
Loved by so many and you never knew how deeply.

Brother Dave, you were just beginning,
You found solid ground.
You were quietly, steadily building on that ground.
Your building was winning the test of time.
Your building would have won the test of time.

Brother Dave, you were just beginning,
Yet there was beauty amidst tragedy.
You were taken in a painless instant.
You were with the friends you loved.
You were near the family you loved.
You were in the mountains you loved.
You were serving the Lord you loved.

Brother Dave, you are now just beginning.
The real loss is ours, not yours;
Ours who knew and loved you here;
Theirs who would have known and loved you here.

Brother Dave, dear, dear Brother Dave,
We will move forward.
We will not forget.
We will see you again.
We will see you again.

—*Jim*

The Counsel of Others

As a grieving father, I wondered if the pain of losing my youngest son would subside. I raised this question with two close friends who several years earlier had lost their daughter through medical carelessness.

"Will the pain lessen with the years?" I asked.

They answered, "Yes, because it gradually changes to gratitude."

Two letters I received carried a similar message. Robert Payton, who had lost both his sons while they were in their twenties, wrote:

> The most powerful consolation for Polly and me has come not from words but from the gratitude we feel for having had so much—for our sons as well as for us. The fullness of your son's 25 years cannot be taken away, nor the memories of the family that was so precious to him. Not the life that was lost, but the life that was won; that's the treasure.

Dr. Alvin Rogness, who had lost his son Paul twenty-five years earlier, said:

> The intensity of pain will diminish, but the loss haunts us to the end. But since loss and grief are a part of life, strangely enough the sorrow becomes a kind of minor chord along with the jubilant majors to give life a new richness. It would be far more difficult if we could not believe that our sons are a part of that great bleacher company, the cloud of witnesses, now cheering us on from the other side.

I found it helpful to ask this question of myself: "Suppose you were told that you could have Dave for only twenty-five years. Would you have him?" My immediate answer was always a resounding "yes." Even as I write this, I realize that gratitude is interpenetrating my pain over losing him.

2 The Cry of Longing

Loneliness is a cry of the spirit.
It does not demand
answers.
It just is.
Piercing, penetrating, unbidden.

A Mother's Cry

Loneliness has continued to be one of my most pervasive cries
during the five years since Dave's death. Characterized by deep
longing such as I have never known before, this loneliness first
broke upon me after the funeral when the other sons and their
families went back to their homes. I would awaken each morning
to a blissful moment when things seemed the same as they had
always been. Then reality would hit, and the enveloping wave of
sadness would wash over me. Dave was gone, and he would
never come back. Never.

Sometimes I would stand outside in the mellow evenings of that
late August and watch to see if he would come driving up in the
old Buick Le Sabre. I could see him sauntering across the street and
up the driveway. He would say, "Hi, Mom," and I—what would I
do? I would run to him and throw my arms around him. But suddenly the quiet street would become bleak, and I would know with
despairing heaviness that Dave would never come again.

In the morning, too, as I made coffee, I would think, *Is that someone coming up the stairs?* (Dave's room was on the lower level.) If I
was alone in the house, I would hold out my arms eagerly. But
there was only emptiness, and always my arms would fall like

dead weights to my side. Once again I had tried to pierce death's mystery and lost.

I would have given much to have cradled Dave in my arms as he was dying, to have told him how much I loved him. Even though that was an oft-repeated expression between us, I would have liked it to have been my final one. This particular longing was powerful in the first months after his death.

On the second of February at about 5:00 in the morning, after I had been lying half-awake for some time, I thought I was in an unfamiliar, somewhat barren place. It must have been that I had dropped off to sleep again, because I became aware that in this room there was someone beside me. At first I thought, *It's John,* but as I looked I suddenly knew it was Dave. I think he had his painting cap on. I said, *Why, it's Dave. Yes. I know it's Dave.*

I said, *I love you, Dave,* and I put my arms around him. I kissed him on his cheek, and it felt cool but not cold. I said, *You know I love you, don't you, Dave?* He gave that little half-smile and gentle nod I knew so well. Then, even as I held him, I felt him slipping away from my grasp, and he was gone.

I felt a warm surge of happiness, but afterward I became very lonely and began to cry. The mood of sadness stayed with me for several days.

I believe that this cry of longing for Dave is intricately woven into my sense of having lost part of myself, as well as part of my motherhood, part of my self-image, part of my self-identity. It stands to reason that when a child dies, a mother is forced to come to grips with aspects of her own identity.

Longing for Dave's Nearness

Dave and I could talk as peers about his struggle to experience the presence of God. I too knew that struggle. It brought us close together.

I missed our conversations about family history, an interest we shared. In a creative writing class at Augsburg he had already written about two of his great-grandfathers. This necessitated correspondence with my Uncle Adolph and a trip to Wisconsin to interview Mert's Uncle Clarence. Dave made a trip to Norway in 1983. There he visited my family on the island of Huglo, the land of his ancestors. He told me of standing on the ferry and seeing the island come into view, when suddenly the significance of his name, *Huglen*, which he had not liked as a child, broke upon him. "I am part of this island," he said to himself. "It is mine." He grinned when he told me that. "I was proud," he said.

Dave was my son, but he was also my friend, and that is part of my longing.

Longing That Begets Loneliness

Often my longing was associated with a time of year or family events or places, but sometimes there seemed to be no special reason. I feared that this longing would stretch to the end of my life. I wrote in my journal:

> Since you died, Dave, I have two levels of thought. I can be in a social gathering and hear what is being said and take part in it. But another lens in my mind focuses in on you, Dave. It's always with sadness and longing. I don't know if people can see it. It's like there is a place inside me that belongs to you, a space no one else can have.

Often I would try to flee from the loneliness. I was keenly aware of this one day when I went to my regular cardiac rehabilitation exercises. In a cooldown at the end of the hour, the therapist often asks us to think of a place where we can feel completely relaxed. Sometimes my mind would creep tentatively to the deck of our chalet in Colorado, but always my muscles would stiffen. No, I could not go there. Most of the time I would be safe going to the ocean, but sometimes that would not do, either. Maybe, I would reason, I can go to a place I knew before Dave was born. But— there was nowhere I could go and be at rest. I wrote in my journal:

Whither shall I flee from the knowledge that
I had you for twenty-five years?
You are forever part of me
Wherever I am.

The first time I saw a video of our church youth group in which
Dave was performing and I realized that according to the script
Dave was going to walk off the scene, I could not bear to see Dave
leave—once again. I stood up and cried, "No, No!" and ran out
of the room. Mert was wise, however, and kept gently suggesting
that I try to watch. He knew I needed to face the reality of what
had happened.

Sources of Loneliness

I could not have predicted which routines and aspects of life
would evoke the greatest loneliness after the death of my son.
Very soon after our arrival home I discovered that it was the
everyday ones—Dave's painting ladder, shopping for groceries,
walking down the alley. It took longer to experience how loneliness was intertwined with seeing the seasons change and the
years go by. This was true also for its penetration into Colorado
vacations.

House painting had been Dave's means of earning money for
college and seminary. On our return from Denver after his death,
even though it was dark, I ran out to the deck to see the painting
ladder, left just where he had placed it the Thursday evening before he left. He knew exactly his painting schedule when he would
return. But he never came back, and as long as I live I will feel
that part of me never came back either.

That first fall I would often go outside, barefoot, in the early
morning, sit down on the step of the walkway, and reflect. *Good
morning, young man with the ladder,* I would say. When my quiet, reserved brother Ray came to Minneapolis the first time after Dave's
death, he walked out to the ladder, sat down, and cried.

Shopping for groceries was a lonely experience. I would con-
tinually be reminded of foods Dave liked or did not like. It was

months before I could bring myself to buy the kind of pork and beans Dave liked in a favorite casserole. It was as though my hand could not reach out to the shelf as I walked by.

In talking with my friend Corrine Chilstrom, I discovered that she shared that same feeling after her son Andrew died. There is something intimate about shopping for one's child. Food is a sacramental symbol of being together around the table.

A day came when I *did* reach out for that can of pork and beans, and I enjoyed eating that casserole again!

Between our house and the church is an alley. That alley represented an unbroken routine of Dave's life. In October, a year after the death, as I walked that familiar path, I thought of how my footsteps too blended into a thousand of Dave's, and I had a curious sense of oneness with him. For a lifetime he made that trek over and over again. And so have I—in the new-fallen snow; in the wet spring rains; in the heat of summer, when the Tarvia almost molds to the shoe; in the autumn, when the fallen leaves swish underfoot.

The Passage of Time

Each year I begin to feel a peculiar loneliness in my spirit as Dave's birthday approaches. A birthday was the day when each son *knew*, "I am important today. This is my day."

The first anniversary of Dave's birthday after his death was particularly hard. The carrot pineapple cake I made turned out perfect, but I cried when I made it.

The birthday is also one of the times I am keenly aware of the passage of time.

Will Dave always be twenty-five? A friend asked me about that one day.

On our bulletin board, just below Dave's picture, I have thumbtacked a poem:

> They shall not grow old,
> as we who are left grow old,
> Age shall not weary them
> nor the years condemn.[1]

I guess that is my answer.

Each season marked the passage of time. I resented the first killing frost, which took the flowers away from the garage where I wanted to look at the snapdragons and say, "Dave saw these, too."

Each year moved me farther away from the time of Dave's leaving us. It seemed as though time was chipping away at our points of commonality with Dave. There were getting to be fewer symbols of life that we had shared together.

Colorado Vacations

The chalet near Buena Vista and the journey to get there from Minneapolis are an integral part of the great loneliness.

Some of our happiest family memories are connected with the long all-night treks across the plains country until we reach the mountains and finally drop down into the Arkansas Valley, where the magnificent panorama of the Collegiate Range stretches out before us.

Dave was eight years old when he first spent a week at Frontier Ranch. It is possible that he and his brother John played in the very ravine where he met his death. In Dave's confirmation autobiography, he wrote at age fourteen:

> Every year our family takes a trip out west to the mountains and for the last several years out to Colorado. I think mountains bring me closer to God. When I climb those massive land shapes which God has created Himself, I can't help but feel closer to Him. There is something so overpowering when, alongside or on top of the mountain, I stand and view for miles around God's intricate creation. Oftentimes when I am feeling down on myself or the Lord, I think of the mountains which stand high, unchanged, for thousands of years, set about and unconquered by man's sinful world, they remind me of God's presence and power and it gives me new strength.

I knew it would not be easy for me to go back to Buena Vista.

The first reality test came that next May, when we went to Colorado for a week. I was surprised to find that simple acts such as stopping in the middle of the night at a service station off the freeway in Nebraska were shot through with painful longing. There had been much companionship in the cup of coffee at the truck stop and in that brief exhilarating run with Pal, our black Lab, to stretch out the muscles for the long drive remaining. As we crossed the mountains west of Denver on our way to Buena Vista, playing the tape of Copeland's *Appalachian Spring* brought out the stabbing pain. I did not want to look at Mount Princeton. The slowest healing from loneliness has taken place as it relates to Colorado.

My son John told me about the first time he flew over the spot where Dave died. He was en route to California and realized just after leaving Denver that, under a clear sky, he would be flying over Buena Vista. In moments it was lying before him—the Arkansas Valley and Mount Princeton itself. He broke into tears.

"But they were not bitter tears," he said. "They were more tears of loneliness, remembering all the special times Dave and I shared in those mountains."

It helped me to hear John say that.

In the midst of all my longing I found comfort.

Sources of Comfort

Nature

Inadvertently I learned about the comfort nature itself can give to a grieving person. Many months before Dave's death in August, Mert and I had planned an October trip to the Maritime Provinces.

"I cannot go now," I said to Mert. For me, all anticipation was gone. There was no sparkle in life, only shades of gray.

Mert, however, encouraged me to rethink my decision. He knew that ever since August 12, I had spoken of a longing to see the ocean. This particular trip would take me to the shores of the Gulf of St. Lawrence on the Atlantic seacoast. The day we stood and watched waves break against the red rock cliffs was like deep calling unto deep in my spirit. The waves are a visible symbol to me of eternity and the power of God.

Now, nearly six years later, that scene on the gulf shore will often flash before me, and I am at peace. We have since spent time on the Oregon coast and sensed again the healing power of the ocean scene.

Obviously, there are thousands of ways in which nature comforts. It may be as simple as looking at the stars or walking in the woods, as sitting beside a tranquil lake or growing flowers in a garden.

Worship and Music

Through worship and music I experience a profound longing for and sense of communion with Dave.

Suddenly something in a church service triggers a memory. For instance, on the first Palm Sunday after Dave's death, I thought of him as a little boy carrying palm branches. I remember him as a high school student singing in the youth choir, or as its director during his college years.

I have a Dave memory of Holy Communion. It is the Sunday of the Twin Cities Marathon in October 1985. Dave and I were driving back from the state capitol, where he had just finished the marathon race. As we turned off Lyndale Avenue and drove by our church, he said suddenly, "Let's stop. There's still time to go in and receive Communion." So off he went. This is a treasured image for me now—Dave kneeling at the altar rail in his running garb.

Often, in worship, my loneliness is related to a divine longing for a reality beyond the life that I now know. Our son Pete told me that such an experience happened for him on All Saints' Sunday, when the church specially remembers those who have died.

In his *Letters of Consolation,* Henri Nouwen says that for him, taking part in the Eucharist is the way that he can be one with his mother, who had died. I have felt for many years that at Holy Communion I receive strength for my spirit. I am my Savior's guest. For me it is also a time when I pray for strength to carry the torch, to write this book, to be part of a caring ministry.

Whenever I hear the National Lutheran Choir, of which Dave was a charter member, I feel that if I look long enough and hard enough, I will see Dave up in the left side of the last tier. Often when the choir sings, the words and music reflect emotions of my grief experience.

Mert and I are regular symphonygoers. Often, during the first three years after Dave's death, the music would evoke vivid memories of the time we walked into the emergency room at Buena Vista and saw Dave's lifeless body. Then my mind would go through the funeral procession, the funeral, and the graveside scene. This may sound morbid, but it was not. It was a hopeful, healing, cleansing time. Perhaps these occasions were essential in my grief journey.

One evening we heard the *Glagolitic Mass* by Leoš Janáček. As we listened to the Kyrie, the Nicene Creed, and the Sanctus, the glorious music seemed to tear my heart out. Another time the crash of cymbals in Prokofiev's symphony was the sound of the thunder right after Dave fell by the tree. And my spirit exulted when I heard Brahms's *Requiem*.

Music has also provided great emotional release for both Normajean and Pete. They told us that on the sorrowful drive back to Minneapolis from the chalet, one of their times of greatest peace came through listening to the entire Mozart *Requiem*, with the beautiful cloud formations on the Nebraska prairie lending a mystical quality to their sadness.

The Grave

For many people cemeteries are not favorite spots to visit. But Dave's grave is still the place where we set aside all extraneous matters and concentrate on remembering him. Mert and I usually talk about many things as we drive down Lyndale Avenue on the way to the cemetery. When we turn west at 36th Street, we inevitably become silent, until we finally come to a stop at the grave.

Being at the grave is a test of our faith. We are forced to look not only at what happened but also at our faith. What do we believe? It is here I think of Jesus and how he cried when he heard the news that his friend Lazarus had died. Was he weeping for the sorrow of his friends Martha and Mary? Was he weeping that death has to come on this earth to destroy family circles and friendships? I think it was for both of these reasons, and it comforts me. I feel Christ's love and care as I stand by my son's grave.

I have memories of my father going to the graveside of a dear friend. If we were traveling, the whole family would go. There he would sing a hymn, and he would pray. He would often tell us something about the person whose memory he was honoring.

Mert and I have done that at Dave's grave. The first few times Mert could scarcely sing. It was an agonizing experience for him. I remember Christmas Eve 1986. We brushed aside the crystaline snow from the bronze marker on which is inscribed the promise in John 11:26: "Whoever lives and believes in me shall never die." We placed roses there from Cousin Johannes Grepstad of Moss, Norway. Dave had stayed at Johannes's home in 1983. We sang the plainsong "Let All Mortal Flesh Keep Silence." But our voices faded away in tears.

Often we reminisce about Dave's gifts to us, and we give thanks.

Because they live in Minneapolis, Jim and Judy and their two children have gone to the grave many times as a family. Four-year-old Christopher, who cannot see, is encouraged to feel the contours of the bronze marker. Dana frequently is the one who places the flowers on the grave. Once, when she was three, Dana insisted on bringing all her dolls along. She lined them up and very seriously introduced them to Dave, one by one. Then she asked her mother, "Do you think Dave was smiling?" Judy said, "Yes, I am sure he was."

With a child's acceptance, Dana would say, "Dave's in heaven." Then very soon afterward, "Is he going to be at his birthday party?"

Christmas

That first Christmas after Dave's death was dreaded by everyone in the family. I understood at last why some people who have sad memories wish they could skip Christmas and wake up, as one woman expressed it, right after New Year's Day.

Remembering my own mother keeping Christmas right after my father's death gave me courage to be sure the first one after Dave's death would be a "real" Christmas. After our traditional Scandinavian meal, we have a family Christmas service. Everyone to the smallest child has a part. For years it has been planned not by us as parents but by our children. At the end is a candle-lighting ceremony. First, the Christ candle is lit. Then each person, beginning with the youngest, comes forward, lights a candle from the Christ candle, and says, "I am lighting this candle because I want Jesus to light my way."

There is a real sense of generations in this candle-lighting ritual. I remembered the year before Dave's death; it was our first together after Tim's return from Africa. I had watched all the grandchildren light their candles. Oldest grandchild Erik finished. There was a pause. Then Dave of the next generation rose to light his candle. I remembered that tears filled my eyes even then. How would we stand it now when his turn came and there was no Dave?

But Tim had been working things out in his mind. Just before our ceremony was to begin, he disappeared and returned carrying a huge split oak log. On the flat, polished side he had made a hole for each family member, burning in below each hole the family member's name.

Tim faced us. It was a tenuous moment. He said, "I am lighting the Christ candle." There it was, in its white pristine beauty. We waited. Then he lifted a white baptismal candle. "This is Dave's candle," he said, lighting it and placing it before the Christ candle.

We cried, all of us, but we also knew there would be no silence or waiting when Dave's turn came. He was already there.

For me, it was like a moment suspended in time. I will never forget it in my lifetime. I said to myself, *Some day my candle will be white, and it will be all right.* That conviction has never left me.

A Father's Cry

> Eric is gone, here and now, he is gone. Now I cannot talk with him, now I cannot see him, now I cannot hug him, now I cannot hear of his plans for the future. That is my sorrow.
>
> —*Nicholas Wolterstorff*[2]

Everyone loved Pal, our black Labrador, especially Dave. As she grew older, her interest in roaming the neighborhood became stronger. There were evenings when we found she had cleverly slipped away. We had no alternative but to go looking for her. Dave, sitting in the front seat of the car, would call longingly out the open window as we drove, "Pal, Pal." His voice persisted as we drove up and down the streets of Richfield. I will always remember the tone of his voice, reflecting an anxious fear over losing his pet. There was no stopping until we had found her and she was safely in our car.

Often as I drive alone in my car, I call out, "Dave, where are you? What are you doing?" It is a cry of longing that I have shouted in my car with tears in my eyes while returning at night from a workshop on helping a congregation start a youth and family ministry. It is a cry I voiced when standing on the shore of the Pacific Ocean, where its vast expanse gave me a sense of eternity. It is a cry I have uttered hundreds of times. Loneliness would engulf me like a fog as painful reminders of his absence surfaced each day.

I discovered that I am not alone in my intense desire to talk with my son again. Dr. Leroy Rouner, in his book *The Long Way Home*, also tells of calling out to his son. He writes, "I would scream to the winter stars for him. I wanted him to come back. At times I cried out for Tim so loudly, I was afraid the neighbors would hear."[3]

Dr. Adolfo Quezada underscores the reality of this cry of longing when he says, "I not only grieve the loss of my son but also the loss of the relationship between us."[4] In a letter to his son, Quezada says,

Missing you is torture to my soul. Yet with all my heart I believe that you are more alive than I am. I cannot wait for a time in some distant future to be reunited with you. I would have it now. I believe you are with me now.[5]

Quezada poses the paradox that I feel so keenly. I recognize that my son is dead, buried in the ground, while simultaneously I believe he is alive, having entered a larger life. This belief gives substance to my longing.

From Death to Life

On Dave's bronze grave marker are etched the words, "Whoever lives and believes in me shall never die."[6] I asked for these words to be engraved because we believe them and, I sometimes add, "fiercely so." Irene and I believe that anyone whose life is centered in Christ "has passed from death to life,"[7] into a life that is never-ending. We take seriously the words of Christ that God is a God not of the dead but of the living, that there is significance in his words to the thief on the cross, "Today you shall be with me in Paradise."[8]

I often reflect on the story of Peter, James, and John on the Mount of Transfiguration. They were able to see Christ talking to Moses and Elijah, who have been out of their bodies for hundreds of years.

I remember the passage from Revelation used as a text at my mother's funeral. It describes the redeemed in heaven as "serving him day and night."[9]

What I am referring to is what Martin Luther called a "spiritual resurrection." Regarding life after death, Luther said, "It is true that souls hear, perceive and see after death; but how it is done we don't understand. If one would say, 'The soul of Abraham lives with God, his body lies here dead,' it would be a distinction which to my mind is mere rot. I will dispute it. One must say, 'The whole Abraham, the entire man, lives.' "[10]

"One day our spiritual beings will be reunited with our resurrected body to enjoy the life prepared for his redeemed."[11]

These words of Luther describe how I reconcile two biblical descriptions—the sleep of death, during which one awaits resurrection day, and the life of a celestial being, during which a person serves God until being reunited with his or her body on resurrection day.

In light of the above, I find myself wondering what Dave is doing in this invisible realm to which Christ and the Apostle Paul referred so often. My cry of longing is to pierce the invisible wall separating us and communicate with him in some way. It is irrational but real. I want to be in touch with him in some way, to sense his presence, to have some idea of what he is doing. I want a glimpse into the unseen world where Dave is living and serving.

Nine months after Dave's death, when I was near Mount Princeton, where he was killed, I wrote this in my journal:

> I feel I have a legitimate complaint. Why, God, am I not given a vivid dream or vision or meeting where Dave appears for a brief time to tell me about his activity? Such communications do occur. Somehow, I look for a contact with Dave while here in the mountains he loved so much.

My expectations were unreasonable, and someone could well add "ridiculous." But they were the intense feelings of a grieving father who longed with every fiber of his being to talk with his son again.

The longing of which I speak was brother John's as well, because he and Dave were "soul mates." They had worked together, played together, shared together. By John's admission, his cry of pain has been prolonged over the years. For him there remains an intense longing for Dave. Some of his dreams reflect this feeling of separation and distance. He may dream of being in a room with Dave but be unable to talk with him. Though he tries to get near him, something interferes. For John, who wants to keep loving Dave, there is a feeling that the personal bond is no longer there.

The Communion of Saints

I wonder about the meaning of the historic phrase confessed down through the centuries in the Apostles' Creed—"I believe in the communion of saints." Does it refer only to those of his people now living on the earth, or does it include communion also with those who have died?

J. B. Phillips, a noted writer and translator of the New Testament in modern English, considers it to be the latter. In his book *The Newborn Christian*, he has a section entitled "Communion of Saints." Here he tells of having experienced the "sense of nearness for a fairly short time" of people who died. He also wrote about C. S. Lewis, whom he had seen in the flesh only once but with whom he had corresponded a fair amount. A few days after Lewis's death, while Phillips was watching television, he saw Lewis "appear" sitting in a chair a few feet away. Phillips noticed his ruddy complexion, grinning face, and glow of health. Lewis spoke a few words relative to a difficult circumstance Phillips was passing through.

A week later, when Phillips was in bed, C. S. Lewis again "appeared" and repeated the same message, which was very important to Phillips. Puzzling over these two experiences, Phillips related them to a saintly bishop then living in retirement. His reply was, "Dear John, this sort of thing is happening all the time."[12]

I agree with the saintly bishop. I have heard similar stories from people I know and trust. Some speak of dreams in which their loved one appears to tell them they are all right. Some speak of the overwhelming sense of the person's presence, even of hearing the departed one speak. Several close friends have told me of having actually seen their loved person and exchanged words. Invariably they tell their story privately, conscious of the fact that today's dominant worldview discredits accounts of the invisible.

Two friends of mine, Dr. Milo Brekke, a research scientist, and Dr. Ben Johnson, a professor of theology, carried out a study to determine the extent to which people have extraordinary experiences that they interpret as communication from a departed loved one. Using a carefully constructed questionnaire, on a given Sunday they queried 2,034 people gathered for worship in one of thirteen congregations in St. Cloud, Minnesota. The results were most striking. A total of 25 percent of these churchgoers claimed to have had a supernatural experience of communication such as a dream, a vision, hearing a voice, or the like. All interpreted their experience as providing evidence of another world.

Other studies have shown similar results. In 1974 Dr. Andrew Greeley asked a random sample of 1,467 people, "Have you ever felt you were really in touch with someone who died?" Twenty-seven percent responded that they had.[13]

Ten years later, Richard Kalish and David Reynolds, through a grant from the National Institute of Health, repeated the study on a sample of 434 persons consisting of an equal number of blacks, Japanese-Americans, Mexican-Americans, and persons of European backgrounds. When these people were interviewed, 44 percent said they had experienced contact with someone who had died.[14]

Desire for Communication

My awareness of people's accounts of dreams, visions, or sense of a presence heightened my desire for some type of communication with Dave, a desire that cannot be stilled. It is like looking forward to phone calls, letters, cards, or visits from a family member. We want to stay in touch, to hear how things are going, and to share in the other's life.

This is how I felt during the years that Tim, Dawn, and their family lived in Dar es Salaam, Tanzania, serving as missionaries. We wanted to stay in touch, to communicate with them.

Now Dave is in another country—one more remote and inaccessible. But where? I can only imagine. When our family gathers for our traditional Christmas service of lighting candles, I imagine Dave is with us. During a worship service at church, I imagine where he might be sitting. At concerts of the National Lutheran Choir, of which he was a charter member, I often search the faces of men in the back row to see if he might be there singing. *Where are you, Dave? What are you doing?* I cry with longing.

I write about this longing, this reaching out for some type of communication, because I have heard of it from so many of my grieving friends. They believe their loved one still sees them, loves them, and is waiting for them. When my daughter-in-law Dawn came into the room where Dave was lying dead, the first words that came to her were, "Dave, when I die, I want you to meet me."

My Study of Scripture

My longing led me into an intense study of Scripture, a study that transported me into another kingdom, another world.

Taking my cue from Christ's description of departed people of faith as being "like angels in heaven" or "angel-like,"[15] I looked up all 275 references to angels in the Bible. For many weeks I would look up each reference, read its context, and then note what it said about angels. It was like coming to know the invisible world that was now Dave's. I became so engrossed in this fascinating—often breathtaking—study that I often lost track of time.

I was surprised to see the prominent role of angels in both the Old and New Testaments. In the Gospel of Luke alone I counted twenty-three references to angels, and thirty-two in the book of Acts. I noticed that most of the writers of Scripture had seen angels, heard God speak, or peered into his invisible kingdom by means of a vision. As I read, I became sharply aware of the prominence given this supernatural dimension in Scripture, in contrast to its muted emphasis in contemporary Christianity. Without question, one does not often hear references to angels, the life to come, miracles, or Christ's return. It is in older hymns and liturgies that one finds these themes accented.

I realize that this longing for communication has its dark side, but I am not referring here to the necromancy condemned in the Old Testament when the people of Israel sought guidance from departed spirits instead of the God of Israel. I am referring only to the God-initiated communications often described in both the Old and New Testaments, such as the dreams of Abraham and Joseph; the visions of Jeremiah, Ezekiel, and Daniel; the angel appearances to Peter, Paul, and the Apostles. On a number of occasions God chose to pierce the invisible wall separating us from his invisible kingdom.

Today the dominant assumption is that God no longer speaks through dreams or communicates through visions and appearances. Dreams are generally viewed as no more than an expression of one's inner needs, anxieties, or wishes. I was among those who formerly interpreted all dreams in this way.

Now I question these doctrinaire assumptions. I believe in prayer and the guidance of God's Holy Spirit, and I wish to be open to his continuous revelation. I do not want to read my Old and New Testaments as a record of God's activity, which no longer takes place.

Heartwarming Communications

Seven months after Dave's death, I had my first gift dream, in which Dave suddenly appeared before me, leaning on a counter as though in an ice cream shop. He was wearing a white shirt, open at the collar. He looked lean, muscular, and in great physical shape. Here he was before me—two feet away, lounging in his usual way. I could reach out, feel his arms, and embrace him. I told him how much I missed him, loved him. He said nothing, but he smiled. I felt very good about seeing him, even though I was conscious of his having died. He was so real. Then the dream ended. I wakened and noted that it was about 4:00 A.M.

The dream gave me a sense of Dave's presence not unlike what John Baillie speaks of in his *Diary of Private Prayer*:

> I thank thee for the many spiritual presences with which I shall today be surrounded as I go about my work. For the heavenly host above, for all the saints, holy and humble men, for my own departed friends and family. Let the consciousness of this holy fellowship follow me whither soever I go, cheering me in my loneliness, protecting me in company, strengthening me in temptation, and encouraging me to do all just and charitable deeds.[16]

An unexpected message came in July from one of Dave's seminary teachers, Pastor Mary Marcoux. She had found a video of his last sermon in her class "Communicating the Gospel." With the video came a typed copy of excerpts from his youth-focused talk. Strikingly, his sermon, given three months before his death, speaks of losing a loved one unexpectedly. What he said came to me as though it were a special message from Dave—a communication for which I had longed.

Bad News—Good News

We have on earth things that we really cherish, that we honor and value deeply. Those things are good things. There's nothing wrong with valuing them. But the problem is this: They can be taken away from us. . . . These things happen. . . . It's devastating. . . .

These things, not just the material things, but people—we treasure people—they too can be gone. Taken away from us because there are accidents, there's cancer, there's heart attacks. These things are part of life. . . . It's true of everyone. . . . Probably all of you have at one time or another had someone that you loved taken away. If you haven't, you will. Now that's not very good news, and unfortunately that seems to be the way about life. If there's anything that you can be sure about it's that there are no guarantees.

Now that's the bad news.

The good news is this:

The things that are of heaven, the things that are of God, the love of Jesus Christ; those things are eternal. Those things are guaranteed. God's not going to be stolen . . . God's not going to die. And more importantly the love of God cannot be taken away from you.

The Apostle Paul, he understood that, and in a letter that he wrote to the Romans he said this:

I am sure that neither death, nor life, nor angels, nor principalities, nor things present, nor things to come, nor anything in all of creation can separate us from the love of God in Christ Jesus.

That is a treasure. That is yours. That's guaranteed. It's protected. My hope is that what you'll be able to do is think about that treasure—the treasure of Jesus Christ—and let your heart grab onto it. And when you have it you have the greatest treasure. It's yours—forever.

A vivid dream almost a year after the first one gave me the chance to do what my heart yearned to do. In my dream I was leading a discussion group in a lounge area. Looking up, I saw Dave enter the room. I ran over to him and embraced him with both arms. I remember saying, "Dave, I've missed you so much. It's great to see you." As I began to loosen my embrace, being conscious of standing in front of a group, I felt his arms only tighten. So I squeezed him again in an embrace of love that lasted a good while. The dream communicated a closeness that gave me joy and elation upon awakening.

Living with the Cry of Longing

Without question, what I am helped most by is my belief system. God's promises, which form the center and structure of this belief system, are a constant source of encouragement and hope. I hold to them tenaciously.

I resonate to the words of psychologist Adolfo Quezada, who writes about his son as having entered the vastness of eternity, an eternity to which Quezada also belongs. Therefore, he could write,

> Your soul, my son, has left the cage of time and space in which I am held. You entered into the realm of total Being where my soul also abides.

Quezada adds,

> It is this fatherhood, this sonship, this earthly relationship to which I must say goodbye. It is to our new communion I must say hello.[17]

Hence, the title of his book, *Goodbye, My Son, Hello.*

As a grieving father, I am well aware of the fact that Dave is dead when I shovel away the snow to clear his grave marker and place a Christmas wreath on his grave. But my belief system tells me that only the body we loved is in the grave. Dave is alive as a celestial being. When I am asked how many sons we have, I immediately answer, "Five." For me Dave remains in the present tense as one transferred to another realm of service.

When I pray for members of my family, I include Dave, asking for his growth and development and that he be informed of our continuing love. I find this in keeping with an older liturgical prayer of the church:

> We remember our friends and kindred who have passed within the veil. Keep us in union with them here.

This union is especially real for me when I share in the presence of Christ through the sacrament of Holy Communion. At that time I believe Dave, now a part of God's invisible kingdom, is also present.

My extended reading and study of Scripture have also proved to be helpful, even energizing. It inspires me, lifts my eyes to the hills of God. I find the descriptive fragments that lie embedded in Scripture both fascinating to read and illuminating. They usher me into the spirit world now inhabited by my son. I become impressed with the oft-repeated promises of God in both the Old and New Testaments that have served as a basic orientation and reference point for the saints who trusted in God.

Less important, but certainly helpful, were the two dreams I found reassuring and heartwarming. Like Rabbi Harold Kushner, I must acknowledge that I have no way of knowing whether these dreams were intimations of reality or products of my own wishful thinking.[18] However, I will not assume they were only the latter.

A time when my cry of longing turned into a shout of jubilation was when, in a worshipful setting, I heard the Augsburg College Choir unfold the Advent story under the theme "Come, Jesus, Come." The glory and awesomeness of his soon return, present in the narrative and classic choral numbers, brought tears of joy. The evening brought to mind the words of T. S. Eliot:

> The beginning shall remind us of the end and the first coming of the second coming.[19]

Therefore,

> We wait for the Word of the Lord as we wait for the rains. Our God shall come upon us like gentle dew. Just as the shepherds of Bethlehem rejoiced at His first coming, we shall rejoice at His second coming.[20]

3 The Cry for Supportive Love

In my mind I sit beside you and give you my hands and
express my compassion.
—*In a letter from Else Mueller, Nürnberg, Germany*

A Mother's Cry

We did not cry out for supportive love that day at 5:00 P.M. when
we were told that Dave had been struck by lightning and was still
alive when the ambulance left the ranch. But we experienced that
most primary of all supports as we waited in the reception room
and saw our two oldest sons, Pete and Tim, across from us. We
knew they were there. And they told us later that, hard as the sit-
uation was for them, they instinctively felt, "Mom and Dad come
first. We have to be here for them." When we stood by the emergency table beside Dave, it was Pete who supported me. On the
other side was Tim holding up his father.

The next afternoon, I felt keenly the absence of family as Mert
and I stood on the sidewalk outside the Denver airport. When
Tim's car disappeared into the traffic line, I felt alone, helpless. My
husband, a seasoned traveler, was beside me. I had flown alone
from this airport a few times myself. But now we were bereft of
those who understood us, who knew why we were still reeling
from our blow. Moreover, we were on an uncharted trip of body,
mind, and spirit.

People in grief have specific needs for love and support. These
are the needs I especially felt.

1. *I needed family to support me.*
My family was there when the crisis came. If I wanted to talk, they
were at the ready. If I wanted to be alone, there were no questions

asked. Not only were my family members "there" when the trial began, they have gone with us down the long road afterward.

2. *I needed people who were immediately aware of what had happened and showed they cared.*

There is a natural trepidation about coming home after a death has occurred. What will it be like to walk into the house?

On our return from Denver, as we approached the stoop by the kitchen door, I saw a container. With it was a little note. My eyes flooded with warm tears as I saw the familiar handwriting:

My dear aunt and uncle,
Now is the time to bear one another's burden.
We wish we could lift some of the grief; I am so sorry but nothing comes to my mouth to say.
This is for breakfast or whatever.
All our love and prayers,
Ione and Mark and all

The note was from my niece, and with it was a pan of homemade sweet rolls.

On the kitchen table was a radiant cyclamen plant: "From Heidi," the note said. Heidi was John's friend, later to become our daughter-in-law. I believe we have had a cyclamen in our kitchen almost continuously since that time. The plant came to us as a message of love and life. It still means that.

This was only the beginning. People did know. They did care in a thousand ways.

3. *I needed people who would take the initiative and help with common tasks.*

For the first few days at least, the shock of death removed my ability to do simple, everyday tasks. I also discovered that a person in shock and grief cannot handle many responsibilities at once. My daughters-in-law told me later that it surprised them that I, the caregiver, could not attend to the needs of others.

I needed people to take over the preparation and serving of food, even to telling me what time I should eat. My sisters-in-law sensed this and surrounded me from the moment I came home. Many friends brought food, sometimes whole meals. I needed people who would take care of the phone, the doorbell, messages, callers. I needed people who could read my body better than I could and say, "You look tired. You'd better rest." After the funeral, a good friend, sensing that I was fatigued, said, "Irene, I'm going to walk you right home," which she proceeded to do, down our alley and right into the bedroom. She literally put me to bed. Like a child, I was grateful.

4. *I needed people to come to the reviewal and the funeral, because I needed their hugs, their touches, their words, their "I love yous."*

The ritual of reviewal was literally our community putting its arms around us. Never until I was part of the trauma of death in my family could I dream of the support that reviewal gives. Our families worried about us. "You can't stand for hours like this," they said. "There are hundreds of people waiting in line." Our families were right about the long line, but they were wrong about our not being able to remain for the entire reviewal. Every embrace, every "I care," renewed our strength.

Once in a while someone would say, "We lost a son," or "Our daughter died when she was sixteen." Mert and I felt a stabbing kinship when we heard that. No more needed to be said. We too belong to that brotherhood and sisterhood of shared pain.

Sensing that our last real gift of honoring Dave was to plan his funeral service, our pastor said to Pete and Tim, "Go ahead and work out the details. I've got a sermon to prepare." Planning every detail of the service was a blessing for all of us, and our pastor let us do it. It was a gift, a support of love.

5. *I needed people who showed love by writing letters, sending cards, telephoning.*

We were grateful for the conscious act of love represented by each person who took the time to call us, write a letter, or send a card. Not once did we set a letter or card aside to wait until a later time when we were less busy. Each one was read eagerly, not once but many times. I have saved all the cards and letters, and not long ago I reread them, finding treasures all over again, maybe taking in the meaning more deeply than the first time.

6. *I needed Dave's friends, youth with whom he had worked.*

I was touched by the expressions of grief from Dave's friends, often shown in unique ways.

One friend, in whose wedding party Dave had been only weeks before, got into his car when he heard and drove more than a hundred miles to see us. He and his wife gave us an enlarged picture of Dave taken at their wedding. I treasure Dave's smiling face on that picture; it makes me smile back. Bob, Dave's college roommate, boyhood friend, and companion hiker in Colorado, was studying in Baltimore. At first when his mother called, he told her that he could not possibly come to the funeral. The morning of the funeral she received a phone call. It was Bob. "I'm at the airport," he said. "There was no other way. I had to come."

Some of the friends, young adults and youth alike, wrote poems or creative essays inspired by Dave's death; others wrote letters telling of some incidents in their lives shared with Dave; others wrote of what Dave meant to them.

7. *I needed people who encouraged me to talk about Dave.*

One day Becky, a young woman with whom I became acquainted through a Peer Ministry program at church, called and offered to go for a walk with me around the Woodlake Nature Center near our home. It was not easy to go that day, because my zest for life had taken a downswing. But Becky was my friend, and I agreed to go.

Almost immediately she said, "I never knew Dave, because we joined the church after he left for school. I'd like to hear more about him." Suddenly there was a sparkle within me. I was eager to talk. There was no subject I wanted to talk more about than Dave. For two hours we walked; I talked about Dave, and she listened. Becky gave me a great gift. I have told Becky many times since that our walk together was a bright spot in the string of days after Dave's death. We who have lost a loved one are hungry to talk about our love.

Not all people realize this need in a grieving person. After a grief session that I led, a young man came up to me to say that his best friend had died two years before, and each time he goes back to his hometown he sees the friend's father, but he still has not talked about the death. "I'm going back now to do just that," he said.

8. *I needed the supportive love of my community of faith, my church.*

With a cordon of love they surrounded us. There were people for several years who regularly would stop me to ask how I was doing. They meant it, too, because they stayed long enough to hear my answer.

A month after the death, I went back to work at our church. I am not sure that I was very effective in my position as director of support ministries, but the warmth of the staff was therapeutic. I did not show as much interest in people as I usually did, because grief often makes a person self-centered. Perhaps that is why a mother in grief cannot help her children in grief as well as she would normally do under other conditions. She has little emotional strength available for anyone else.

Working at church meant that I led grief groups, caring ministry groups, and a "You Can Help with Your Healing" group. It did not take me long to realize that I was being ministered to as much as I was ministering. Small groups are a positive support for one who is grieving.

9. *I needed supportive love from others who had lost a child.*

Strange as it may seem, the people who told us they had lost a son or daughter were like rays of hope for tomorrow. I was touched deeply by the large number who shared our experience and took the time to tell us.

There was the elderly Pastor Hjortland, who shared briefly with us as he went through the reviewal line. "I lost a son when he was in his twenties," he said. "He was a seminary student, too. I want to tell you about a verse from Scripture that has since meant a lot to me. It's in Hebrews 11:2: 'He died, but through his faith he is still speaking.'" Mert and I have thought gratefully of that verse many times.

There were Ruth and Phil, who eleven years before had lost their teenage daughter, Mary, by drowning. They told us that for the first three years they could not even look at her pictures, but Ruth said, "Now the memories have a sweetness about them. They don't hurt like they did. We can laugh about humorous incidents in which Mary was involved." I remember marveling about that. Was it possible I could ever again laugh about Dave without the knife turning inside? But it was a supportive statement, something to hang on to. There were Marion and Les, whose twenty-one-year-old Paul was killed in a plane crash. I saw the pain and tenderness in Marion's eyes when she said, "Paul would have been forty-two today." I wanted to believe that I, too, would follow along with each birthday. My eyes, too, would fill with tears. My memories would not fade.

There were Norma and Ray, who had lost their Reid as a young man. They spoke of family gatherings where there was always a special longing for him to be there. I liked to hear that.

There was Kay, with whom I had walked the lonesome road after her Mary died. Kay prepared me for some of the loneliness and pain. She also showed me by her life and spirit that one could survive and come out with meaning and purpose for life. She wrote:

> These are strange days. I know—I've been there. I can't make an offer to make it all better. I only know we are carried until we can stand alone. Then, we reach out to others. . . . When we falter, we're carried again. . . . I can't sit and wait for tomorrow when all things will be made whole. . . . Then I become useless so instead I have to produce while I watch for tomorrow. You will find the way to follow and it will become a blessing to all who know you.
>
> *Kay*

A Father's Cry

From the depth of a father's
love
Flesh of his flesh
Did the pride in his eyes show
When he held you in song?
Music and song.
—*Tim Strommen*

Men are not supposed to cry. For that reason, a man's cry for supportive love may seem inappropriate. But it was my cry.

Grief broke on me with great force the first hours after losing Dave. To use the words of Jeremiah, "My eyes became a fountain of tears."[1]

I felt very vulnerable that night Pete and Tim drove to Denver to tell John of the tragedy and bring him to our chalet. While they were gone, I was desperate with anxiety over a possible accident in which I might lose more sons. The same fear plagued me in Minneapolis as I awaited the three-car caravan from Colorado. An enormous feeling of relief flooded my being when I heard their cars enter our driveway.

My need for supportive love showed also in the events I especially remember with appreciation.

Expressions of Love

I fondly remember the pastor's visit to the chalet that hellish night of Dave's death, the friends who came from Trail West Lodge the next morning to clean our chalet and encircle us lovingly with prayer, the breakfast given our family before we sorrowfully left for the airport. Why are these expressions of love so memorable? Because I needed them.

I will never forget walking up the ramp after flying from Denver to Minneapolis and seeing Judy and Jim; my brother, Luther, and his wife, Helen, there to meet us. From that time on, Irene and I were surrounded by a family whose physical presence and love gave the support for which I cried out in the anguish of my grief.

I worried about the public reviewal, as did Irene. Already short on sleep and emotionally drained, I feared an exhausting day. But I discovered the power in being loved and supported. The people who came—friends of Dave, friends of our family, members of our congregation—embraced us, wept with us, and expressed their love. Rather than feeling emotionally drained at the end of the evening, I felt energized by the love given us.

I had not been aware of the comfort flowers can give. One reason may be that as a boy I heard my father, a pastor, rank the importance of memorial gifts far above that of flowers. But flowers ministered to my spirit. After Dave's funeral, we selected certain ones to fill our home as symbols of the resurrection and new life. They were such a solace to our spirits that we resolved always to have fresh flowers in our home.

I discovered also how much comfort is given through the written word. In the past I seldom read the verse on a greeting card. Now I read every word and eagerly looked for written comments. I treasured the letters and cards we received and read each one several times. What I especially appreciated were the many people who said they would pray for us each day. Never before had I felt such a great need to be prayed for.

In the past, people thought of me as one well able to care for myself. Now it was different. My whole being quietly cried out for support and love. I was discovering what it means to be part of the body of Christ. When one suffers, others suffer with you. I was the one suffering.

The funeral service, which I dreaded, lifted my spirits. The promise of eternal life came alive in the music, talks, and singing. An inspirational climax came as the Augsburg College alumni choir sang Larry Fleming's new composition, "Blessed Are They." This anthem takes on an emotional intensity when the black spiritual "Give Me Jesus" breaks in to create a joyous climax. A sense of exhilaration in my Lord overwhelmed my grief. I was ready to witness my most dreaded event—committing Dave to a grave.

My First Christmas

A time when I felt most vulnerable were the days prior to our first Christmas after Dave's death. For weeks I had been told how festive seasons intensify one's grief. Christmas for some is a time they wish they could avoid. For me it became an opposite experience, but it did not start that way. The day before Christmas, when Irene and I stood at Dave's grave, I was overwhelmed by the realization that a graveyard would always be part of our Christmas—this sacred, happy family time. We sang several songs with Irene carrying the tune, because my eyes were blurred with tears and my whole being bowed over in sobbing. Then we prayed, thanking God for Dave. Again I was overwhelmed by the sense of loss, with our son gone and in a grave.

When we began our festive Christmas Eve dinner, surrounded by sons, daughters-in-law, and grandchildren, I felt as though I had been cleansed by the tears. Others felt the same cleansing and were free to talk about Dave as though he were present. For me Christmas was a time when I gave Dave back to God. I reflected this in the closing prayer I gave at our dinner:

> Father in heaven, this night is especially sacred, tender, and fraught with meaning for us. David's chair stands empty; his plate carries no food. He is with you, with the angels, with the many loved ones who are part of the cloud of witnesses looking at us from the other side of life. You know how we miss him—how easily our tears flow. The depths of feeling we experience tonight cannot be expressed in words.
>
> In the midst of our tears we cling fiercely to your word. And because we do, we believe David continues to live, to serve, to sing, to talk, to remember, to see, and, significantly, to love us still. Though our eyes cannot see him, O God, we believe he sees us, hears us, loves us more than ever. Give us an increased sense of reality as to his presence with us. Increase our confidence in your promises.
>
> I confess, dear God, that I have held on to Dave as though he belonged to us. He is yours, because we gave him to you in holy baptism.

In a letter of condolence, Pastor Hoover Grimsby picked up this theme of belonging when he wrote,

> Dave did not really belong completely to anyone here. He belonged to the King. His life was loaned to the world, the community, to his place of work, to his Church, and most particularly to you, his loved ones, for this period of years.

The Fellowship of Fellow Sufferers

Through Dave's death we joined a unique fellowship with others who have also lost a child. I could sense their understanding and empathy, a result of their having experienced what I was now going through.

One reason conversation between fellow sufferers is so precious is that each can resonate with the other's grief, even years after the death. I noticed that after a month or two had passed, people tended to avoid the subject of Dave's death, either to spare me further pain or thinking it was now past history. For me silence about Dave was awkward, because his death remained prominently in my mind. Therefore, to break the ice and make conversation, I often found myself bringing up the subject. I always appreciated being able to talk about him.

I needed to talk about my grief lest it harm me. I noticed that grief was eroding my patience. Irene, who characterized me as always the harmonizer, now noticed a feistiness in my personality. I became easily impatient with myself and with some of my associates. Driven by grief, I needed supportive love.

The Embrace of Love

Through my experience of grief I came to realize how much I needed the support and love of family, friends, and faith. I needed to hear people say they were with me in my grief, that they recognized how painful it is. I needed someone to listen to me while I told them about Dave and our loss. The pathway to a healthy bereavement is lined with people you can talk to and lean on.

One thing I learned during this time of sorrow is how much I have needed the embrace of love and the spoken words "I love you." These are now always a part of the good-byes we give members of our family when they leave our home.

Husband-Wife Conversations

Irene was an enormous support, because we were able to talk about our feelings, reminisce about Dave, cry together, and pray together. His death united us in a deeper bond.

Here we were helped by what we learned to do during an earlier crisis. Some thirty years earlier Irene had struggled with a depression, "postpartum blues." It came when we were under stress—financial and emotional—to raise a family while I was trying to complete my doctorate in counseling psychology. We learned then how much it helped both of us to spend time, even hours, talking through unresolved feelings. We found that it was the best way to relieve her depression.

Author Joan Bordow expands this idea of husband and wife communicating with each other in stressful situations such as the death of a loved one. She offers the following suggestions in her book on coping with the death of a child.[2]

- Let discussion be open-ended, allowing time for "all there is to say."
- State the intention and willingness to hear the other express feelings.
- Let each spouse talk with no rebuttal until all desired feelings have been expressed.
- Ask what kind of support he or she wants.
- Avoid interruptions, such as the phone or doorbell.

Parents need to give each other time and space to process and integrate what has happened in their own individual lives during this stress period.

The Sense of God's Presence

The death of a loved one can drive one away from God. In my case, it drove me closer to him. I found his promises to be channels of comfort, his way of reaching into my life.

Becoming vulnerable through the suffering brought on by grief makes it possible for God to change one for the better. This I hoped would be true for me. Hence, in my prayers I found myself asking that my love for those around me might expand, my gratitude for all that is good might increase, my insight might deepen, and my faith in his promises might intensify.

The danger is that losing a sense of God's presence can create a "black hole" in one's spirit. This is what happened for our grandson Andy. Ten years old at the time of Dave's death, Andy was the most volatile of all the grandchildren in expressing emotion. He was the most angry in destroying his "fort." He cried inconsolably for several days. No attempts to help him seemed to give relief. During the week after the funeral, Pete, his father, began to suspect there might be a tie between Andy's grief and the fact that Dave had been his godfather, a role Dave had taken very seriously. He and Andy were special companions. During a conversation with his dad, Andy revealed that he felt he had lost not only Dave but God as well.

The following Sunday the pastor at our church conducted a brief ceremony in which the role of godfather was transferred to Andy's Uncle John. This seemed to be the beginning of Andy's reconciling himself to what had happened, because his crying stopped. Pete followed up on this with long talks and walks with Andy.

Andy maintained this sense of God's presence by reading each night for over two years a devotional book given him by Dave. This helped him feel close both to his Uncle Dave and to the God he revered.

4 The Cry for Understanding

> The hardest lesson of all . . . [is] to accept what one cannot understand and still say, "God, thou art love. I build my faith on that."
>
> —*William Barclay*

A Mother's Cry

Early in the journey of grief came the cry for understanding. For me, it was also a cry for being able to accept what had happened and to integrate my grief in a healthy way. I liken it to a cry for bridges between mourning Dave's death and finding significance and meaning because of it.

Questions with No Answers

In a letter from Bettye and Howard, who lost a ten-year-old daughter through suffocation in a snowbank in their own front yard, were these words:

> The sense of mystery is overwhelming as we walk this path. It overtakes our desire to comprehend. We are left only with acceptance.

I suppose the question "Why?" came to me most often in the first months. I can honestly say I never asked, *Why me, God?* Somehow I had no illusions about that. No, I was asking, rather, Why could not the lightning have struck ahead of or behind Dave?

Sometimes I would have the mental image of myself with outstretched hand holding Dave back from taking that last step. Why could the lightning not have traveled through a nerve along the side of the body, as it usually does, and come out at the lower extremities? Then he might not have died.

The toughest of all were questions like these: God, why did you allow Dave to be taken—Dave who had committed himself to serving you? Dave who felt that you had given him unique gifts for working with kids? Did you not need him here, God? What was the meaning of the year in which he struggled and made his decision to enter the ministry? What was the meaning of his joy at making the right decision? My mind cried out for understanding.

I have asked other questions, too. They really do not demand an answer, but they reflect my attempts at piercing the mystery of death.

The Break in Childlike Trust

I like to study the Bible privately. For years I have done this, often using good commentaries, meditating, journaling my thoughts and sometimes my prayers. It is a "my God and I" time. I found the words of O. Hallesby in his book *Prayer* to be a satisfying description of this relationship:

> In our fellowship with God in prayer . . . there are things which . . . can be and should be formulated in words. . . . But there are also things for which we can find no words. . . . That is the way it can be when we are praying. It can be just resting as a child would do on a mother's lap. "I have nothing to tell you," we can say to God. May I lie here awhile and rest?[1]

On August 11, the day before Dave died, I made the last entry in my prayer journal for several months.

At the funeral itself and for several weeks afterward, the veil between the unseen world and my own life on earth seemed gossamer thin. The transcendent glory of God was intensely real, but not the subjective aspect, not the intimacy I had known. Especially after family members had gone back to their homes, I became aware of this change.

All through my life, prayers have risen spontaneously within me. Now when such a prayer would begin, a knife twisted inside and I would quickly pass on to another thought. Even though I participated in group studies in church, it was clear to me that I shied away from sitting down alone with my Bible and journal. Just thinking about it made my body stiffen. This troubled me. I discussed it with my friend Dr. Bill Hulme, who offered this: "Maybe it's as though you're a little angry with God right now. Maybe you feel God has let you down."

It was an idea that at first I wanted to pass over. I did not want to admit that to God or myself, but on October 20, six weeks after the death, reluctant as I was, I wrote this:

> Dave, I feel sort of angry at God at times for taking you. It hurts me to write this [I remember how difficult it was to pen those words, and I observe now that I could not speak directly to God. I addressed Dave.] I feel disillusioned, as though I can't pray for protection as I used to. I want to believe God called you, rather than that your death came as a result of a willy-nilly whim of nature which God did not care to control. I *know* God was with you always, *that* I have never doubted.

I have pondered a great deal about this attack on my childlike trust. Some years later an incident helped to clarify it for me. Our grandson Christopher loves us very much and is beautifully demonstrative about it. Last year we had been absent on vacation and had not seen him for two months. Eagerly we approached him, expecting the usual glad response. When Christopher heard our voices—he cannot see—he began to walk quickly toward us. Then suddenly he stopped and deliberately turned away, making a wide arc around us. For a full half hour he refused to come near. He had been hurt and was a bit angry, too, because he could not understand our absence. Twice he made a tentative move, then turned back again.

I believe I did the same to God. My love and faith were still there, just as we knew Christopher's feelings for us had not disappeared. I certainly knew that God understood me and loved me. But my feelings had been hurt, and I wanted God to know that and suffer a little.

I was tentative in going back to that close relationship we had had, just as Christopher had been tentative. On November 10 I wrote that I had resolved to begin my Bible studies again, but on January 3 I wrote, "I haven't started my Bible studies yet."

God knew that my heart was longing for the old relationship in which I could figuratively lie down as a child in God's lap, just content to be there, saying nothing. God just waited.

On April 1, 1987, this is the entry in my journal:

> I want you to know, Dave, that this morning I began to record thoughts from my study on the Gospel of John and I'm glad. Your death has had a deep effect on my emotions, to say the least. I can't tell how much on my actual beliefs. But one thing I know, I am praying for help to accept, to place this whole event and succeeding months in your hands. They are a mystery. I cannot know why. I do know God never left you. I know *nothing* can separate us from God's love. A bolt of lightning cannot. Sorrow cannot.

What caused me to reestablish a close relationship with God? I cannot say that I know. Certainly there was no sudden flash of understanding. It may be as hard to figure out as what caused Christopher to come back to our arms.

I believe, however, that the Holy Spirit, who has promised to enlighten and strengthen me, was operating all the while. In my journal through those months it was clear that I was feeling out the tenets of my faith, as it were, and becoming convinced that they had not changed.

I believe that the step I took on April 1 was one of forging ahead in the storm. New strength was given me to go through.

How Do I Let Go?

Every book I read on grief and loss stressed the importance of "letting go." The phrase bothered me. Did it mean—and here was a pain-loaded question—that I would have to give up my earthly loving of Dave to be free of that beloved bond? Did I have to put him on the "back burner," as one writer described it?

I did not want to let go of my young man, with all his hopes and dreams. I was his mother. I felt that if I did not hang on tightly enough, the memories might dim and fade. I did not want him to forget me, either. I wanted to be important to him. The memories hurt, but I feared that if the pain went, I would lose Dave.

I wanted to push time back, maybe to the morning of August 12. I wanted to live in the days when there was no fracture in our family circle. I wanted Dave coming home for Sunday dinner, telling me what was happening in his youth work, in his seminary classes.

One evening in October we were at the home of friends with whom we have been meeting regularly for over a decade. It is a friendship circle that has become for each of us at various times a support group. I expressed to them how I was afraid of letting go and asked what they thought I should I do about it.

Bill, who had lost a daughter in her twenties, was gentle in his reply. "I wouldn't worry about it now, Irene," he said.

Bill was wise that evening. He probably knew I had to work this out for myself.

About that time, too, I read Wayne Oates's *Pastoral Care and Counseling in Grief and Separation*. In his concluding chapter I saw these words:

> In grief we shrink back to nostalgia—we try to make time stand still, to keep things as they were, to go back to a more secure and familiar place by a way we have always known.

How well I knew about that feeling! But I read on:

> Faith provides another alternative . . . faith is the commitment to grow through events like bereavement . . . by reliance upon a living God who is always renewing life through faith's response to the claims of growth.[2]

That challenge did not, of course, take away the struggle to accept and integrate what had happened. But I tucked it away in my thinking. Within the first weeks, for instance, Mert wanted the brothers to look over Dave's clothes and take for themselves what they would like to wear. I thought it would be very difficult for me to part with them. But when I saw Pete, Tim, Jim, and John lovingly handling the shirts, even the suits, hesitating, wondering if they should really use them, I knew it would be right. They took some of his books that they could use. This too was eminently right. More and more I wanted to accept what had happened and go through the process of grief in a healthy frame of mind.

In early 1988 I recorded what I felt was a statement of my understanding at that time of "letting go":

> Reality is that you, Dave, are forever in the Eternal Kingdom. Maybe letting go is being able to thank honestly for the memories and believe God will give me grace to live with that.

I felt a release after writing that statement.

But I added this afterthought: "Are we important to you any more? Do you love us? I don't want you to be sad, but I want you to care."

That statement reflects, I think, that the grief journey is not a steady march forward. As I see it in my own experience, it is a mosaic of emotions and insights, sometimes zigzagging across each other, sometimes running parallel, sometimes coming one after the other in a neat pattern. Two steps forward, one step back.

There are still times when it worries me that it is harder for me to look at old pictures of Dave than it was at first. I ask myself, "Is this natural for a mourning mother? Or am I a person who just can't let go?"

It is not so long ago that I went through some of Dave's old clothes in his closet. I found myself hugging a pair of torn jeans and then, after placing them in the wastebasket, retrieving them.

I like to walk down into his room, now only occasionally occupied by an overnight guest or by four or five grandchildren sleeping in there at one time. They seem to like the idea of sleeping in "Dave's room." And that warms my heart.

I can finger lovingly the artifacts from school and college. I note again the books he was reading. I have even framed the flier advertising Dave's painting business. I have framed his posters from drama productions at college, high school, and church. His paintbrushes are still where he left them. So are his yearbooks.

Bridges to Understanding

In my cry for understanding I found these concepts helpful.

Opposites Coexisting

I was bothered by seemingly contradictory emotions. How could I laugh when I was feeling so sad?
How could I be resentful of what had happened and yet accept it?
How could I let go and still hang on?
How could I believe and doubt in the same breath?
How could I actually experience deep joy, as at the birth of Christopher, and yet feel the unutterable pain of having lost Dave?
How could I say in the sixth month of mourning that I understood more now about the love of God, more of what it means to be thankful?
One bridge to understanding for me was to accept the idea that opposites can coexist.

Balance

I have always been thankful for the saving grace of humor. I believe the ability to laugh at myself and with others is one of life's balances over against grief and pain. This kind of laughter comes easier for me again.

My perspective on our family has become balanced again, too. No figure looms larger than any other. I ponder the gifts Dave gave to me, but I ponder also the inimitable gifts of each son. I feel more deeply privileged than ever to be a mother, a mother-in-law, and a grandmother.

In this balance is the treasure of love and companionship with Mert, my husband of nearly fifty years. This grief journey has taught me qualities in myself I did not know, or at least not in depth. It has also taught me qualities in Mert that I did not know in depth. The wrenching, bleeding experience for both of us to lose Dave made us more aware of our gifts to each other. We learned patience in a new sense. We learned we did not always grieve alike, or rather that we did not always work out our grief in the same way. But I treasure the fact that we allowed each other space to grieve as it was best for us. This granting of freedom to each other was not always done automatically or without differing opinions.

It may be that a person in the stress of grief becomes more intensely himself or herself. I was more inward in expressing emotion during the first months after Dave's death. This could mean that I am more reserved by nature than I often appear to be, or that I was off balance in my time of grief, and one aspect of myself loomed larger than it usually does.

I have often been curious about the role of shock in the experience with death, especially sudden death. I am sure I was mercifully protected from some intensities of mental anguish for a longer period than Mert was. He experienced the hoarse, wrenching sobs within minutes; that was not true of me. I wondered if I would suffer a sudden time of tremendous jolting, but my grief experience seems rather to be gradual and ongoing. Sadness and mystery were pervading emotions and still are, though to a lesser degree, even now. At first there seemed to be more passivity about my spirit. Yet—and here we come to those opposites coexisting—I began to fight right away, too. I would face the storm; I would grow; I would endure.

I am quite sure that our children have come to resonate with us, their parents, in a different and deeper way because of the struggles they have observed us going through. We as parents have come to understand our sons and daughters-in-law in a different way, too.

This experience has taught me that our family can face pain, utter disappointment, fears, doubts together. Age really does not matter. Love does.

Events of my life have assumed their proper perspective. After Dave died, my father's death, once the most cataclysmic, moved into the far background. Now it once again is seen in its rightful place in the panorama of my life. My open-heart surgery, once the greatest experience of facing my mortality, also receded as though it had never happened. It has been finding its place again. Not long ago my mother died. Her death is still both real and unreal, but it will take its place, too.

Spiritual Renewal

Probably the single greatest instrument in helping me integrate Dave's death into my faith and life is the Bible study, journaling, meditation, and prayer that have characterized many early morning hours during these years. Through these, God has provided windows for me to see the larger picture, sometimes through a writer, sometimes through my own reflections.

I cite here an insight from William Barclay[3] for which I am very thankful, one that involved the broader meaning of the word *endurance*. It implies, Barclay wrote, more than "bleak acceptance of suffering." Endurance implies triumphing over suffering.

Very early I vowed I would endure my trial. But I thought of it as biting the bullet, thrusting my head forward into the storm, letting the waves and the billows go over me. That was *enduring*.

Through my reading, I realized the word *endurance* could have far deeper implications for the rest of my life.

The ability to endure enables a person to pass the breaking point and not break but go on to new strength, an inner transmuting. Barclay's conviction about endurance no doubt deepened through his struggle with grief after losing his daughter Barbara, who as a young woman drowned in the North Sea.

In the first throes of grief I was turned off by the idea of a grief experience being a chastening. I told God that I wanted to grow, but not that way. I had to relearn that God speaks to me through difficult times, "trials of testing,"[4] as the Scriptures often call them. I realize that if I had let resentment and rebellion become the dominant theme of my grief, I would not have been able to hear the voice of God that has been so life-giving to me in my sorrow. I have a renewed conviction that hard things can have great results for good.

A Father's Cry

> During those hours I cried. It was then I clenched my fists and
> asked the inevitable question, Why?
>
> —*Adolfo Quezada*[5]

I was in Palm Springs three months after Dave's death, attending
a conference led by evangelist Leighton Ford. Because I had read
the book *Sandy*, which he and his wife had written telling about
the loss of their son, conversation between us came easily. His son,
a runner and committed Christian leader, had died during an operation on his heart. When I told him about Dave's sudden death,
two big tears rolled down his face. For the next thirty minutes,
we walked the footpaths of the spacious motel grounds, talking
about our sons and telling of our search for answers. One of his
final remarks I will always remember: "I have come to realize that
I understand God less but trust him more."

Indeed, trust in God's providence and wisdom is basic to the
Christian life. It is enough to believe that God had his own compelling reasons to allow Dave's death. But my mind continues to
puzzle over aspects of his death; wondering questions continue to
surface.

For some, the cry for understanding may be short-lived. For me,
it remains a persistent, puzzling cry, one that I have come to realize is shared by others. Dr. Leroy Rouner, whose twenty-five-year-
old son died while mountain climbing, wrote these words:

> My head still needed to know what an accident is and what
> to make of God's power. I couldn't accept the idea that this evil is
> beyond God's reach.[6]

When Dr. Ronald Knapp interviewed mothers and fathers of
155 families who had lost a child, he found it rare for parents to accept the loss of a child as an act of "fate." Most tried to arrive at
some way of understanding the death.[7]

The cry for understanding persists even though my heart rests in the knowledge that God loves me and wills only my good. I find encouragement for this pursuit in the words of Proverbs:

> If you cry out for insight and raise your voice for understanding, if you seek it like silver and search for it as for hidden treasures; then you will understand the fear of the Lord, and find the knowledge of God.[8]

Though still involved in my search, I am willing to share my thoughts and identify what has helped me most with this cry.

Grappling with Unanswerable Questions

God's Role

I cannot silence the cry for understanding by simply saying, "It was God's will that Dave die. God caused it." The psalmist does not say, "My tragedy comes from the Lord." He says, "My help comes from the Lord."[9] Nor can I say, "It was a random act of an imperfect nature. There was nothing God could do about it." That leaves me with a theology of a helpless God.

Neither of the above statements presents a position that I can accept, yet both contribute to what I find meaningful. I am caught in a dialectic in which two opposites coexist. They pose a dilemma that my net of meaning is too small to contain.

I am not uncomfortable, however, with a dialectic, because there is one in the center of my belief system. It is expressed by the Latin phrase *"simul justus et peccator,"* which means I am simultaneously justified by God and a sinner. It means I am forgiven, redeemed, a child of God, and holy in God's sight. At the same time I am a person who sins daily, am prone to unbelief, and daily need to repent and be renewed.

I find this idea of a dialectic reflected throughout the Bible in many paradoxes. Christ is born of a woman and born of God. His Church is both human and divine. How can both be true? That is the mystery.

In my groping effort to understand, I do not find myself blaming God for Dave's death. Nor do I see the event as a punishment or as something evil. Though I call Dave's death a tragedy, I still view it as an event in which God was redemptively present to accomplish his loving purposes.

Questions of "Why?"

And yet I ask, Why the seeming waste? Why take a promising youth leader when so few are available for a critical area of need? Why waste his years of preparation, his training, the countless hours, weeks, even months of time he spent working with young people? Why did you motivate him with such a strong sense of call into a youth ministry?

His uncle, Bishop Elmo Agrimson, posed the issue well when he said,

> Here was talent abundant: a respectful son, congenial brother, understanding friend, compassionate counselor; loyal to Christ and his church. Why does this happen to one so committed, so young, and so promising? Where is the providence of God?

If I could look back twenty-five years from now, I might see how Dave's death fits into God's great design. What seems meaningless now I may see as meaningful then.

I say this as one impressed by a new science called "chaos." In almost miraculous ways scientists are finding patterns and structures within the random and seemingly chaotic events of our world. Although highly mathematical in origin, chaos is a science of the everyday world. Marvelous discoveries of form and amazing symmetrical patterns are being found in such unpredictable events as the behavior of weather, the flow of oil in a pipe, the way people make decisions, the formation of snowflakes, the flow of a river, the distribution of earthquakes, and the action of the human heart. The focus of many scientists today is shifting from a preoccupation with what one molecule does to a preoccupation with what millions of them do.[10]

As I read about how scientists are discovering an order that underlies the seemingly chaotic, I think of the Old Testament and the design underlying its seemingly endless rebellions, battles, and destruction of towns. At a chaotic time, Isaiah envisioned a new order in which the wolf and the lamb feed together and the lion eats straw like an ox. At a time when the people of Israel called down the wrath of God by refusing his guidance and were being resettled in other countries, Jeremiah predicted that Israel would never cease as a nation. His message was clear: God, working through a chaotic history, will bring about a new order, a new existence.

I find it satisfying to think that God can work through events that seemingly make no sense, events he may not have wanted but that he yet uses to accomplish a future purpose.

My probing for meaning, I discover, is something very personal. I do not want a professional theologian to tell me how to interpret Dave's death. I do not want other people to press their explanations on me. I react when a writer espouses a certain position as though any other is theologically naive or untenable.

But I do appreciate learning about the struggle of others, the questions they have faced, and how their cry has been met. No doubt much of my intense personal search will give way one day to a resignation described so eloquently in a letter by a dear friend. Twenty-one years after the burial of her daughter Naomi, then in the prime of life, Gracia Christensen was able to write,

> As I stood with Tom by Naomi's grave, for the first and perhaps only time, a tremendous peace filled me. The old tugging "whys" were no more. There was only an incredible joy in her, a gratitude that she had been born and that she had lived her abbreviated years so richly. And that her life continues!
>
> I suppose we shall never cease wondering "what if . . . ?" But I just wanted to bear you witness that the years do bring an acceptance that bear[s] God *no* grudge. The black stone of grief, miraculously, grows smooth with our long handling of it. As Samuel Longfellow's hymn so beautifully puts it:

Thou leadest me by unsought ways,
And turnest my mourning into praise.
Thanks be to God!

The Realm of Mystery

My questions, however, focus not only on "Why?" but also on events surrounding Dave's death. Consider several most puzzling questions.

Dave had been memorizing Psalm 139 and discussing a portion of it with Judy Young, a counselor from Bayport, the day he was killed. It was his favorite psalm, because it describes so well the constant presence of God:

You know when I sit and when I rise;
You perceive my thoughts from afar.
You discern my going out and my lying down,
You are familiar with all my ways.
Before a word is on my tongue
You know it completely, O Lord. (vv. 2, 3)

The passage says God knew Dave was jogging over to the site where a lightning charge was building up to explode. He saw it with love in his heart for Dave. If Dave had sauntered over instead of jogged, would the bolt have struck the ground before he came? He was in a lower "hanging ravine," considered the safest place on the side of a mountain. Was his arrival at that tragic moment a random happening or one under God's control?

The psalm also says, "In thy book were written, every one of them, the days that were formed for me, when as yet there was none of them" (v. 16).

The New International Version translates the verse in this way: "All the days ordained for me were written in your book before one of them came to be."

Does that mean that Dave had but twenty-five years allotted to him? Does this foreknowledge of God predetermine the years of a person's life? I find this thought both awesome and puzzling. I recognize that the doctrine of predestination is one way by which theologians explained how God rules the world.[11] My stepmother, Ve, a few days before her death, had a dream in which she was summoned by a voice that she identified as that of either her father or her husband. Upon awakening, she began preparing for her death, which she viewed as a new adventure. She called the pastor of her church and said she would no longer be able to serve as parish caller. Because of her congestive heart condition, she shortly afterward entered the hospital for care. As part of her preparation for death, she requested that my oldest brother come to her room so she could make sure he knew where she kept the list of valuables she was bequeathing to family members. The same day my brother had visited, Irene was talking with Ve and had just reached out to remove her glasses and place them on the table beside the bed. Ve was talking about plans for the next day. Then very quietly she breathed her last.

Was her dream of being summoned to the next life prompted by God, her guardian angel, ESP, or simply an unconscious response to the knowledge of her condition? How much do persons in God's unseen world know about impending events? How did Old Testament prophets come to know the future? Isaiah wrote what reads like an eyewitness account of Christ's suffering and death, centuries before it happened.

I was aware of the dreams that had puzzled Abraham Lincoln a few days before his death. In his dream, he descended stairs in the White House, hearing sounds of grief. Soon he saw a casket being guarded by soldiers. When he asked who had died, he was told the president had been killed by an assassin.

The night before his assassination, Lincoln had another dream. This time he dreamed of being on a sailing vessel that was taking him to a dark, shadowy shore. What caused these dreams?

Though explanations for these phenomena are beyond our realm of understanding, we cannot stop searching for a rationale. I say this because people I know well had dreams and premonitions prior to Dave's death.

Strange Premonitions

On Sunday morning, two days before Dave's death, our family occupied one long pew in Faith Lutheran Church in Buena Vista. Directly in front of Normajean sat Lisa Stahlecker, the camp nurse at Frontier Ranch, one of the first to give CPR to Dave two days later. For some unexplainable reason, Normajean found herself overwhelmed with tears near the end of the service. She consciously did not want to be introduced to Lisa after the service and quickly left the church.

On that same Monday, the eleventh of August, Honnie LaDue back in Richfield had a troubling premonition of tragedy when seeing the Oak Grove youth leave Minneapolis for a work project in Denver and then a week at Frontier Ranch. Honnie, a good friend of John and Dave and a determined supporter of the youth group, was acquainted with premonitions. One such experience occurred for her in Germany during World War II, when she was with her family in an air raid shelter during a bombing raid. Agitated to a point of desperation by a sense of disaster, she compelled her family to move to another air raid shelter. Seconds after moving, the family saw their first refuge devastated by a bomb. The same sense of uneasiness troubled Honnie as she said goodbye to John, who was serving as the church bus driver and leader of the youth group. Before he left, she said, "John, here is my 800 number at work. If you have any trouble, call this number."

That Monday evening three people also had troubling dreams that they later connected with Dave's death. Here is what Rollie Larson, a friend of our family, told his wife the morning before Dave's death:

> In my dream I was in a house in a mountainous area. Suddenly there were two tremendously loud explosions, maybe about one second apart. I went to the window and opened the drapes. At some distance (maybe a mile) I was horrified to see an entire mountain burning. Stick-like tree trunks were burning. A charred airplane fuselage was in the foreground at the base of the mountain. I thought that certainly nobody could survive such a disaster.

At this point I thought to myself, "This is like a bad dream; but this is *not* a dream. This is real."

I hurried around, trying to find my hiking boots. I needed them because the task of helping would be wet and muddy. Surely I would know some of the people aboard that plane—they were arriving for some kind of meeting or conference that I knew about. The disturbing thought was that someone I know is aboard that airplane, and there is no way anyone could survive that explosion and fire.

That same Monday evening, between 2:00 and 4:00 A.M., Rollie's daughter, Jane Wipf, a good friend of Dave's, had a frightening dream that she described the next day in her journal. Her dream involved a flash of light like a big light bulb exploding. It caused her to wake in a panic and to arouse her husband, Mike. Concerned that the dream might be an omen involving their four-year-old son, Tommy, she asked Mike to see if he was all right. He was. Mike, a medical doctor, said he had never before seen her in such panic. Jane adds, "And I've never had a dream like that."

The same night, Polly, one of Dave's youth group at Frontier Ranch, dreamed she had seen Dave walk through and out of the camp and later heard that he had been hurt so he would not return.

I do not understand these events, because Irene and I had no premonitions, no dreams. Even at the time Dave was struck by lightning, we were driving comfortably back to Buena Vista with no thoughts of impending doom.

The Birth Watchers

These premonitions, if they can be called that, are puzzling and disturbing because they are associated with impending tragedy. But there may be another side to these premonitions—a happy side.

It might be that people inhabiting God's invisible realm and having advance knowledge of impending deaths await people's entry into God's kingdom as we await the birth of a child. That is the position of George Macdonald, the spiritual father of C. S. Lewis. He saw death and birth as two sides of the same coin. He wrote,

> The couch of the dying, as we call it, is surrounded by the birth watchers of the other world, waiting like anxious servants to open the door to which this world is but a windblown porch.[12]

I have heard many stories from reliable sources of how people when dying have seen loved ones who preceded them in death. The welcome they are given causes their face to light up in rapture, joy, and excitement.

I stood at the bedside of my aged father, who was in a coma, slipping away from the land of the living. For a long time he had not been able to raise his head from a pillow without help. Suddenly he awakened, sat up in bed, and began peering at something at the other end of the room. What he saw with wide-open and knowing eyes caused his face to take on color, aglow with an eager smile. What he saw had energized his whole being for a scant minute. Then he sank back into his coma and a few hours later was gone.

It may be that citizens of God's kingdom (who according to Christ rejoice when a sinner repents) also know when a person's numbered years are ready to end. It may be that this knowledge, like radio waves, is picked up by the occasional person on this earth who resonates to these vibrations. An event that for us brings death and tears means birth and a joyous welcome for the citizens of heaven.

Added confirmation for the idea of "birth watchers" comes from Dr. Raymond Moody, a psychiatrist who interviewed 50 people from a sample of 150 who had reported near-death experiences. In his book *Life After Life,* he reports that a number of those he interviewed told of meeting friends who had already died.[13]

Dr. Osis, a Latvian psychologist, also pursued this phenomenon by means of three studies of deathbed visions. His information came from doctors and nurses. In his study of one thousand reports of deathbed visions, he discovered that the most common experience of patients shortly before death was seeing a friend who had died and being welcomed by them. These reunions, according to the medical observers, were characteristically joyous.[14] This thought has been a blessing to me as a grieving father. Now when I write letters of condolence, I often include a copy of George Macdonald's poem about the birth watchers of the other world.

Evocative Dreams

Since Dave's death our family and friends have had dreams that have been both meaningful and evocative.

Nick, a friend with whom Dave often exchanged records and tapes, had a dream one month after Dave's death. He dreamed he was in the youth room of his church in Bayport with the people who had taken the Colorado trip. He noticed a phone like a receptionist's phone in the room. One of the youths gave him a number and told him he should call it. After dialing the number, he heard Dave answer with beautiful soft music in the background, like one might hear at a garden party. Then he heard Dave say, "Nick, don't get wrapped up in worldly things. It's so much more beautiful up here."

In a note to me, Nick wrote, "I interpret the dialogue as God trying to tell me not to get so wrapped up in worldly possessions such as money and clothes."

Several weeks later, Normajean had a dream in which she saw David in jeans and a blue shirt. With a smile on his face, he was saying the names of each grandchild as though praying for them. To Normajean the dream brought comfort, because it suggested a new role for David—that of a "guardian angel" who prays for the children.

Two months after Dave's death, Siri, one of the grandchildren, then nine years old, had a dream so vivid that she ran upstairs to tell it to her parents. Here is her dream as recorded that day by her mother:

> It was morning at our chalet. I was going to have breakfast. I saw Uncle Dave eating a biscuit. I gave him a hug. Then I told everyone else he was here. Then he led everyone outside and said, "I'm sorry I didn't get to say good-bye to everyone at the

rodeo." He hugged everyone and then said good-bye and disappeared. There was only one thing different about Dave: his hair was standing straight up like he had a punk haircut.

Puzzling to me was her reference to Dave's hair. Though I knew from a medical report I received later that lightning had caused his hair to stand straight up, I chose not to share that information with anyone. How did it become part of her dream?

The same morning, Judy had a three-part dream so powerful and vivid that it left her in tears. Here is her account of the second part:

> The next episode of my dream took place on David's wedding day. He looked very trim and youthful, full of health. He was dressed in an elegant black tuxedo with a white shirt. The atmosphere was festive, and preparations were under way for the wedding. The next thing I recall is that David and I began to dance in ballroom fashion. His movements were extremely fluid, smooth, and airy. I was surprised that David could dance like that, and I said, "David, I didn't know you could dance so well." He replied, "Everything is easy for me now." It was as if at that moment I became aware of what was happening—everything crystalized for me, and I seemed to now understand that David was with me dancing, but not exactly in the physical, earthly body I recognized. At that point I clearly recall looking directly at David's face and into his eyes. His eyes were a paler blue and looked translucent to some degree. As I looked at his eyes, I said, "David, I miss you," to which he replied, "I miss all of you." That ended the second episode of my dream, which was so vivid that it seemed real in some sense. I knew I would not forget the content of my dream.

About this same time, Jim Schreyer, Dave's close friend, had a dream so compelling he thought it was real. In his dream, Jim, serving in Dave's place as youth director, was in the youth room with those who had gone to Colorado. Suddenly Dave appeared. Incredulous, Jim asked, "What are you doing here? I don't get it."

Dave answered, "I've never really left." Then he proceeded to explain why he could still be there and why it seemed natural to the kids. In the dream, the explanation made perfect sense to Jim. When Jim awakened, his first impulse was to look for Dave. Our son John had a dream that began unfolding with his talking to Irene in our kitchen. When the phone rang, John answered it. He heard a voice say, "This is Dave, your brother. I thought you would like to hear from me." Overwhelmed emotionally, John was unable to talk. When awakened, he felt he had actually talked with his brother. It was a thrill that lasted for several days.

How does one understand these dreams? Should one dismiss them as the product of unfulfilled wishes or a video of one's imagination? Is it possible that these dreams could be stimulated by an outside force, that they are something other than a grief reaction? We do not know; we can only wonder.

There is good reason, however, to assume that dreams are not created only by our wishes, needs, or anxieties. An article in *American Psychologist* (1985) by Irvin Child of Yale University reports on research on dreams carried out at the Maimonides Medical Center.[15] Fifteen different studies are cited of controlled experiments in a sleep laboratory at the medical center. In these studies people are wired so that observation of their brain wave patterns will indicate when they begin dreaming. Once an REM pattern is seen, a person in another room is asked to concentrate on a randomly selected picture. When the dream is ended, the person is awakened and asked to describe the dream. Significantly, the dreams tend to resemble the picture chosen at random. The results could not have happened by chance.

Such evidence does point toward a sensitivity of the human spirit to outside influences. One need only think of Pilate's wife, who was forewarned in a dream that Pilate should have nothing to do with Christ's death. It does seem to suggest the possibility that dreams can be instigated by an outside reality, good or evil. One ought not dismiss all dreams as being only a creation of our inner needs and wishes.

To use the words of Dr. Alvin Rogness, the theologian, "Who are we to say the veil that separates the living from the dead may not be a very thin one?"[16]

Mystery and Paradox

Death does provoke spiritual questions, and these became my cry for understanding. I found it helpful to grapple with the questions of "Why," God's role in a tragedy, and life after death. Rather than unsettle my faith, the experience of searching for answers has served to deepen it, to root my faith more firmly in the soil of trust. Rather than being repelled by the mystery, paradox, and puzzling aspects of the Christian faith, I find myself awed by its profundity.

Today, however, my questions of God are less insistent. I realize that some of them may be no more meaningful than my asking how many hours there are in a mile.

What I found most helpful was focusing on a God who mourned with me and who wanted me to learn and grow from my heart-rending experience, a God who could be described in the following paraphrase of John 3:16:

> God so suffers the world that he gave up his only Son to suffering.[17]

It is this God who is changing my mourning into thanksgiving.

I have found comfort also in the vivid dreams reported to me by members of our family. They come as gift dreams, because each one tells something about Dave that is like a communication from the other world.

I am content not to press the issue further but to agree with J. B. Phillips, writer and translator of the New Testament, whose vision of the life to come through a near-death experience was of "breathtaking magnificence." He wrote,

> No doubt it is best for us now that (the unseen world) should be unseen. It cultivates in us that higher perception that we call faith. But who can say that the time will not come when, even to those who live here upon earth, the unseen worlds shall be seen?[18]

5 The Cry for Significance

You do not honor the dead by dying with them.

—*Ingrid Trobisch*

A Mother's Cry

In the early years of this century, out in southwestern North Dakota, lived Enos Nesse, a shy, faithful man who belonged to Mamre, a country church. Enos had a severe speech impediment. In all his years of attending Bible studies or prayer meetings, no one heard him speak. When Enos died, he left five hundred dollars to the church in appreciation for its blessings to him. The people of Mamre chose to use this money for purchasing a memorial bell, with the name Enos Nesse cast in the iron. It always moved me to think that this man who had been denied the gift of speech in life was calling people to worship over those prairie hills through the resounding voice of a bell.[1]

I remember a student at Augsburg College who left for the army when World War II began and was sent overseas to Europe. Word came that he had been killed in combat. This was hard news for all of us on campus, but I was puzzled by the response of his parents. In the midst of their pain and sorrow they sent a gift of money to the college in thankfulness for their son. They wanted him to live on with meaning through the lives of other young men and women.

My cousin Bjarne Sveinsson in Oslo, Norway, lost his three sons, all in young adulthood. Then his wife, who had been in a wheelchair for many years, died. I learned from other cousins that after the bitterness of his sorrow, Bjarne determined to live the remainder of his life in service to his neighborhood. He invited the lonely, elderly, and sick to his home; he chauffeured them to social gatherings in the neighborhood. When we met him, we found a jovial, perceptive, warm person. His deep grief had become an occasion for finding significance through caring about others.

Closer to home, I have a dear friend who fought despondency and poor health after losing her husband and thirty-one-year-old daughter within a short time. Nevertheless, my friend Kay decided to continue working with children in her home and at church by leading voice and bell choirs and teaching piano. Some of her students would not have been able to get this experience had it not been for her generosity and interest. For Kay the teaching was life-giving.

Living for Others

I am challenged by what Cousin Bjarne, the Augsburg student's parents, and my friend Kay have done. I too want my life to have significance that is in some way related to the life of my son. Very soon after Dave's death, I wondered if God had something special He wanted me to do.

My cry for significance was answered almost immediately in quiet ways through working at church and in the everyday life of my family. But eight months later this happened in a much greater way, when our little grandson Christopher was born. For me, he was like the "wheat that springeth green" in the winter of my sorrow. He was almost four months premature, weighing less than a pound his first month. He had not only the handicap of undeveloped lungs but also the struggle of battling five different infections: two staph, two fungus, and one RSV. His life at times hung in a precarious balance.

Christopher literally lifted me out of myself into the realm of caring intensely for someone else. More than that, by his own fierce struggle for life, he challenged me to wrestle in prayer for him. My first spontaneous burst of praise to God after Dave's death came when Christopher survived his first bout with infection. Christopher's parents, Jim and Judy, have allowed me to be one of the caregivers for this little person. During many hours of singing to him, my own voice has come back. For a long time after Dave's death, singing would seem to tear my heart out. Now it does not.

The desire to have something meaningful come out of Dave's death is not unique with our family. A cousin wrote that she and her husband have taken a long look at work and their family life, restructuring it to give maximum time to the things of greatest importance.

In a spontaneous way, a project with both personal and wider significance came into being because of Dave's love for running. He was training for his fourth marathon when he died so suddenly. Lewis Workman, a veteran runner and father of one of Dave's friends, declared on the day of the funeral that he was going to "run for Dave." Dave's brothers Tim, John, and Jim took the challenge and began a grueling six weeks' training and also ran in his place. They and eight others finished the run.

The event caught the attention of the media, and the brothers had a chance to present the cause before a television audience. Each year since then a group has run, with proceeds going to the David Huglen Strommen Endowed Fund. The runners wear T-shirts reading simply, "For Dave."

"Marathoning with meaning" is what Dave's friend Karsten calls it.

It has had great meaning for Tim. He told us that during the six weeks he trained for the Twin Cities Marathon, he felt that Dave was running beside him. During these times Tim found himself talking to Dave. When tired on a long stretch, he would chant Dave's name as he ran. Even now, after five years, Tim indicates that he still experiences the same emotions as he runs. Tears came as he finished the marathon in 1988, because he had a strong feeling that Dave was there at the finish line.

I struggled to find my own area in which I could contribute to the ongoing significance of Dave's life and dedication to mission. It seemed important to me that, if I were to "carry the torch," I choose some area that fit my capabilities and interests, had integrity as far as my relationship with Dave was concerned, and was in keeping with Dave's interests.

Peer Ministry: Reaching Out

In my longing to do something with meaning in Dave's memory, I thought of Peer Ministry, a program that teaches youth to be aware of another's pain and needs and trains them to reach out in friendship and caring.

Dave had been trained in this program in both high school and college. As a youth director, he had been eager to have his volunteer leaders trained so that he could begin Peer Ministry in that fall of 1986. I was teaching his group in the summer of 1986. One of the last conversations Dave and I had was after a Peer Ministry session on July 25.

That night the group had been assigned one-to-one conversations on "a decision I made at some point in life, why I made it, and how it changed my direction." Dave told me on our drive home that if there had been time, he would have liked to share with the group about the decision he had made to enter the ministry and how it had affected his life.

I remember saying, "Oh, Dave! I talked so much you didn't get a chance!"

He made nothing of it, but I have remembered it many times since, mostly because I regretted that I did not respond that night by saying, "Tell *me*. I'm interested."

When we arrived home, we continued our conversation sitting in the car, and I shared some personal frustrations of my own. Dave listened carefully, and then I heard him giving me feedback on what I had said, helping me to clarify my thoughts. Dave was not only my son that night. He was my peer minister.

Though I had taught this program for a number of years in my congregation, I received encouragement to become involved in the Peer Ministry program on a larger scale through the Augsburg Youth and Family Institute. Blessings have come into my life through contact with youth and their leaders, persons who have a great sense of mission in caring for and reaching out to others.

Writing My Story

A friend suggested "journaling to Dave" as a means of therapy, a means of letting me look at my feelings and sort them out. My little spiral-bound journal became my friend. Not only did I take it on long trips, but also I often would tuck it in a shopping bag when I knew I might have a waiting time somewhere. My journaling has been a blend of Bible study reflection, prayers, writing how I feel, and describing some of the events of my life. I have been able to look more clearly at some of my mistakes, my self-centeredness. I have also had the thrill of seeing some new truths.

When Mert first suggested that we write a book about our grief experience, I said I could not. I was sure that going through each page of my journal, reliving again the painful events of that day in August and the days following, would be anything but therapeutic. I thought it would take more emotional energy than I could afford to spend.

But little by little I persisted, because deep inside of me was a desire to write about this, the most profound sadness of my life. It became part of my cry for significance.

Writing this book has been a healing experience for me. As I write this, I am reminded of my friend Bettye, who wrote:

> Time does not heal. Prayer heals. The Holy Spirit heals. You choose to heal. Time only covers the event. Time only puts distance between us and the event.

In *As Seeing the Invisible*, author D. T. Niles[2] speaks of how often in the events of God's history there are the overturning and then the restoration: the Calvary and then the Easter. What happens in the grand scale of God's history can happen in our individual lives—there can be the overturning by death followed by the restoration, the Easter.

A Father's Cry

> My motivation now, more
> than ever, is to be for
> others where and when
> I'm needed. I feel
> compelled to ease the
> pain of others.
>
> —*Adolfo Quezada*[3]

Until Dave's death I was always future-oriented, assuming that problems have solutions, difficulties can be resolved, closed doors can be opened. Then I discovered that death cancels possibilities and the chance for hoped-for changes. With death, facts become unalterable.

Yet within me continues to well up a cry that Dave's shortened life be continued in some way, that his decision to serve, gained after struggle and prayer, not be buried. At his death, I felt keenly the need to see something develop that would be an extension of his ministry, that would bring meaning to a promising life wasted by death. Since then I have come to realize how universal this cry is.

Art Linkletter, whose daughter died during a drug experience, gave his energies and considerable talents to an antidrug campaign.

Otto Frank, father of Anne Frank of World War II fame, published her diary with the offer to correspond with any adolescent seeking greater confidence and hope in life.

A mother, incensed over the senseless death of her child caused by a drunken driver, started the organization known as MADD (Mothers Against Drunk Drivers). This militant organization, now national, has been a powerful force in effecting legislation that places severe penalties on those who drive while intoxicated.

A Minneapolis schoolteacher, grieving over the death of his father, a pastor who loved music, decided to memorialize him with a pipe organ. Over the years he saved money for this project until he was able to pay the $100,000 needed to install a pipe organ in the church his father had served.

Extending Dave's Ministry

The night of Dave's death I talked with son Jim, miles away in Minneapolis, about establishing an endowed fund at Augsburg College for a Youth and Family Ministry that could continue Dave's mission. Originally, Dave had planned to be a high school teacher and coach. However, while practice teaching, he became aware of the contrast between working with youth in a congregation (which he had done for a number of years) and in a public school, where he could not share the life-transforming message of Christ. After taking a year out of school to ponder his decision, he enrolled in the seminary.

A few months before his death, Dave, as a youth director, represented Bethlehem Lutheran congregation, Bayport, Minnesota, at a meeting to consider forming an Augsburg Youth and Family Institute. Its purpose would be to assist congregations in addressing the burgeoning needs of youth and parents. It was a ministry Dave wanted to make his life career. Already in his work with youth he had become acquainted with the parents and visited them in their homes. The idea of an institute that worked for strong, life-shaping families appealed to him.

In my conversation with Jim, I asked, "Could an endowed fund be established at Augsburg College that could ultimately fund a professor's chair in Youth and Family Ministry?" The answer received next day from the college was "Yes."

Days later I saw words that expressed my cry for significance. They came in a letter of condolence from my friend and long-ago colleague Dr. Wilton Bergstrand. He had included a four-line couplet that said what I felt so keenly:

> May the music of his death
> Be the sound of marching men
> May his heart a thousandfold
> Take the field again.

That is what my heart yearned to see: a thousand young men and women taking Dave's place in a congregation's youth and family ministry.

A dear friend, Dr. Barbara Varenhorst, who had flown in from California for the funeral, reflected the same conviction in a letter she sent to us:

> I frequently think about Pastor Prasek's funeral sermon that although we can't answer the question, Why did God let this happen? we can ask, Where do we go from here? I believe God will use it to further youth work in many ways we can't even comprehend. I believe, too, that David will know and rejoice in it.

We have started an institute at Augsburg College whose purpose is to nurture in youth and families a commitment to Christ and a life of service. Its goals are to train laypersons and professionals for a youth and family ministry, to create resources for this new ministry, and to provide consultation to congregations for bringing about the changes this new model of ministry requires. The project involves the writing of foundational books and the development of curricula for the college training programs. It involves the development of resources for congregations that open up new possibilities in a vital ministry with today's generation.

At times, when the responsibilities of launching this new endeavor seem especially demanding, I wonder if my efforts to launch an organization are primarily grief-driven. However, in quieter moments I realize that my need to be doing something significant in memory of my son can be a healthy and appropriate response to grief.

I found affirmation for this point of view from a friend, Sue Salasin, who had recently lost a close friend. She writes,

> It is often said that to have our children die before us is the cruelest blow of all. . . . Shelby tells me that you are working on a memorial. I feel that it is the only way to achieve a transformation of grief into growth. It brings a special joy unlike any other.

The Need to Do Something

A parent's need to see something of significance rise out of tragedy again became apparent at a lunch I had with the bishop of the Evangelical Lutheran Church in America, Herb Chilstrom, and his wife, Corinne. They were grieving over the tragic death of their twenty-year-old adopted son, Andrew, a freshman at Gustavus Adolphus College, who had taken his life. The question uppermost in their minds was this: What good can come out of Andrew's death? The answer we arrived at centered in the possibility of a pioneering research project. Its purpose would be to bring new understanding to a puzzling area, the troubling dynamics within many adopted adolescents. The Chilstroms' cry for significance became a driving force. With memorial monies and a small grant they helped secure, we were able to write a research proposal that secured a large grant for a study of adoptive families. Together we want the study to give meaning to a tragic death. Truly, the cry for significance expresses itself in a need to do something.

Transforming Grief into Growth

This cry for significance and need to do something encourage me to look beyond my grief to a service-oriented cause. Doing this is important for maintaining my sense of well-being and eagerness for new adventures and countering the natural tendency to become self-centered. Too often people who have lost a loved one lose also their zest for life. With a loss of purpose and desire for life often follows a strange vulnerability to sickness and disease.

Our decision to start an Institute for Youth and Family helped me past a preoccupation with my pain and longing to provide in its place a compelling sense of goal and purpose. This project, fraught with possibilities and meaning, has helped me cope with my grief and has provided an answer to my cry for significance.

Though a foot race may seem insignificant, it is impressive how important the first Marathon Run for Dave became for me. Its purpose was to raise funds for an endowment established at Augsburg College for training students in a youth and family ministry. As I identified with the runners, I felt that something meaningful was being done for an important cause. Standing at various points along the marathon course, I cheered for the eleven red-shirted runners who were running for Dave. What I did not realize was how powerfully grief still held me in its grip then, six weeks after his death. When driving to the last cheering point in the race I lost my sense of spatial relations and for a while was hopelessly lost in a city I knew well.

Probably the most helpful cause of all was the rare privilege of entering into a battle for the life of a grandson. Told that it is important for a child prematurely out of the womb to be touched and talked to, Irene and I went almost every day to the hospital to give him company. I would stick my hand into the tiny isolette so Christopher could clutch my little finger with his hand.

These visits, at times stressful because of Christopher's condition, caused our prayers and concerns to go beyond ourselves and to center on him. He became literally our purpose and cause as we prayed for his life, growth, and development. We imagined that Dave probably joined Christopher in his little isolette, whispering words of encouragement and challenging him to show that a preemie given less than a 5 percent probability to live can make it. When Christopher's birth announcement finally came, three months after his birth, he was introduced as a child of prayer. It was a joyous time, because he had become for me, family, friends, and congregation a symbol of resurrection and life. Today he is a healthy, sight-impaired, strong little boy who is deeply attached to his grandparents, and we to him.

We do not know what good comes from a death, but Leighton Ford, who lost his son, Sandy, is convinced that life does blossom from death, that it is God's way. He believes the words of John 12:24 are more than a metaphor; they present a literal truth:

> Unless a grain of wheat falls into the ground and dies it abides alone, but if it dies, it will bring forth seeds.

Epilogue

Today Irene and I both wish to make the most of our remaining years—to bring comfort and encouragement to others as we have been helped. Without question our grief experience has intensified life for us, sharpened our sense of mission, and made us grateful for each additional year we are permitted to serve.

For us, Dave's death brought God's invisible realm closer and made the separating veil seem thinner. At the same time it has increased our sense of awe over the mystery of life and the life to come.

The intensity of our pain has now subsided, and gratitude for having had Dave as a son has increased. Irene says it well:

> Memories do not sear and burn as much.
> Events in life have assumed their proper perspective.
> Healing does not mean love has gone with the pain.

One never recovers fully from grief. Now, almost six years after the death of our son Dave, there are times when the grief over losing him overwhelms us with sadness or erupts into tears that come suddenly like a spring storm and are gone as quickly as they came. These times almost always come when we are alone, meaning our expressions of grief have become strictly private.

Because such grief is rarely seen in public, the uninitiated accept the widely held myth that cries of grief soon end with the passage of time. They do not. The ministry of supportive love needs to continue.

In spite of our persisting grief, we agree with the philosophy of life found in the message Dave had taped on his church office door in Bayport, Minnesota:

> Life is a miracle—and the right to live is a gift. It's wrapped in a ribbon woven of dreams—and whether you are very young or very old—life is filled with wonder and surprises.

Notes

Chapter 1: The Cry of Pain

EPIGRAPH. Adolfo Quezada, *Goodbye, My Son, Hello* (St. Meinrad, IN: Abbey Press, 1985), 45.
1. Luke 2:35.
2. Harold S. Kushner, *When Bad Things Happen to Good People* (New York: Avon, 1981), 64.
3. National Academy of Sciences, *Bereavement: Reactions, Consequences and Care* (Washington, DC: National Academy Press, 1984), 152.
4. National Academy, *Bereavement*, 81.
5. Judy Tatelbaum, *The Courage to Grieve* (New York: Harper & Row, 1980), 9.
6. Matthew 5:4.
7. Quezada, *Goodbye, My Son, Hello*, 32.
8. Leighton Ford, *Sandy: A Heart for God* (Downers Grove, IL: Intervarsity Press, 1985), 171.

Chapter 2: The Cry of Longing

1. John McCrae, *In Flanders Fields*.
2. Nicholas Wolterstorff, *Lament for a Son* (Grand Rapids, MI: William B. Eerdmans, 1987), 31.
3. Leroy S. Rouner, *The Long Way Home* (South Bend, IN: Langford Books, 1989), 90, 112.
4. Quezada, *Goodbye, My Son, Hello*, 37.
5. Quezada, *Goodbye, My Son, Hello*, 52.
6. John 11:26.
7. John 5:24.
8. Luke 23:43.
9. Revelation 7:15.
10. Hugh Thompson Kerr, ed., *A Compend of Luther's Theology* (Philadelphia: Westminster Press, 1943), 241.
11. Kerr, *Luther's Theology*, 239.
12. J. B. Phillips, *The Newborn Christian* (New York: Macmillan, 1978), 213–14.
13. Morton T. Kelsey, *Afterlife: The Other Side of Dying* (New York: Crossroad, 1985), 97.
14. Kelsey, *Afterlife*, 98–99.

15. Mark 12:25.
16. John Baillie, *A Diary of Private Prayer* (New York: Scribner's Sons, 1949), 93.
17. Quezada, *Goodbye, My Son, Hello*, 46.
18. Kushner, *When Bad Things Happen*, 28.
19. T. S. Eliot, "A Cultivation of Christmas Trees," in *O Frabjous Day! Poetry for Holidays and Special Occasions*, edited by Myra Cohen Livingston (New York: Atheneum, 1977), 170–71.
20. Augsburg College Vesper Program, 1991. Augsburg College, Minneapolis, MN.

Chapter 3: The Cry for Supportive Love

1. Jeremiah 9:1.
2. Joan Bordow, *The Ultimate Loss: Coping with the Death of a Child* (New York: Beaufort Books, 1982), 52.

Chapter 4: The Cry for Understanding

EPIGRAPH. William Barclay, *Letters to the Corinthians*, rev. ed. (Philadelphia: Westminster Press, 1975), 199.
1. O. Hallesby, *Prayer* (Minneapolis: Augsburg Publishing House, 1931), 147–48.
2. Wayne E. Oates, *Pastoral Care and Counseling in Grief and Separation* (Philadelphia: Fortress Press, 1976), 78–79.
3. Barclay, *Letters to the Corinthians*, 170, 212–13.
4. William Barclay, *Letters to James and Peter*, rev. ed. (Philadelphia: Westminster Press, 1976), 42–44.
5. Quezada, *Goodbye, My Son, Hello*, 25.
6. Rouner, *The Long Way Home*, 107.
7. Ronald J. Knapp, "When a Child Dies," *Psychology Today* (July 1987): 60–67.
8. Proverbs 2:3–5.
9. Kushner, *When Bad Things Happen*, 30.
10. James Gleick, *Chaos* (New York: Penguin Books, 1987).
11. Rouner, *The Long Way Home*, 108.
12. George Macdonald, *The Musician's Quest*, edited by Michael Phillips (Minneapolis, MN: Bethany, 1984).
13. Raymond A. Moody, *Life After Life* (Atlanta: Mockingbird Books, 1975), 48.
14. Kelsey, *Afterlife*, 91–92.
15. Irvin Child, "The Question of ESP in Dreams," *American Psychologist* (November 1985): 1219–30.
16. Alvin N. Rogness, *Appointment with Death* (Nashville, TN: Thomas Nelson, 1972), 11.
17. Wolterstorff, *Lament for a Son*, 90.
18. Phillips, *The Newborn Christian*, 119.

Chapter 5: The Cry for Significance

EPIGRAPH. Ingrid Trobisch, "The Price of Loving," *The Lutheran* (March 29, 1986): 14.

1. J. Elmo Agrimson, "The Voice of a Silent Saint," in *Christmas Echoes* (Minneapolis: T. S. Denison, 1955), 84.
2. D. T. Niles, *As Seeing the Invisible* (New York: Harper & Brothers, 1961), 151–52.
3. Quezada, *Goodbye, My Son, Hello,* 6.

Bibliography

Bittner, Vernon J. *You Can Help with Your Healing*. Minneapolis: Augsburg Publishing House, 1979.

Bordow, Joan. *The Ultimate Loss: Coping with the Death of a Child*. New York: Beaufort Books, 1982.

Bozarth, Campbell. *Life Is Goodbye, Life Is Hello*. Minneapolis: CompCare Publications, 1982.

Davidson, Glen W. *Understanding Mourning: A Guide for Those Who Grieve*. Minneapolis: Augsburg Publishing House, 1984.

Donnelly, Katherine Fair. *Recovery from the Loss of a Child*. New York: Macmillan, 1982.

Erdahl, Lowell O. *The Lonely House*. Lima: C.S.S. Publishing, 1989.

Ford, Leighton. *Sandy: A Heart for God*. Downers Grove, IL: Intervarsity Press, 1985.

Gleick, James. *Chaos*. New York: Penguin Books, 1987.

Graham, Billy. *Facing Death and the Life After*. Waco, TX: Word Books, 1987.

Grollman, Earl A. *What Helped Me when My Loved One Died*. Boston: Beacon Press, 1981.

Heavilin, Marilyn Willett. *Roses in December: Finding Strength Within Grief*. San Bernardino, CA: Here's Life Publishers, 1986.

Hulme, William E. *Pastoral Care and Counseling: Using the Unique Resources of the Christian Tradition*. Minneapolis: Augsburg Publishing House, 1981.

Jewett, Claudia L. *Helping Children Cope with Separation and Loss*. Cambridge, MA: The Harvard Common Press, 1982.

Kelsey, Morton T. *Afterlife: The Other Side of Dying*. New York: Crossroad, 1985.

Knapp, Ronald J. "When a Child Dies." *Psychology Today* (July 1987): 60–67.

Kübler-Ross, Elisabeth. *On Death and Dying*. New York: Macmillan, 1969.

———. *Questions and Answers on Death and Dying*. New York: Collier Macmillan, 1974.

Kushner, Harold S. *When Bad Things Happen to Good People*. New York: Avon, 1981.

Manning, Doug. *Don't Take My Grief Away*. San Francisco: Harper & Row, 1984.

Miller, Mary C. *Devotions for Those Living with Loss*. Chicago: Covenant Publications, 1991.

Moody, Raymond A. *Life After Life.* Atlanta: Mockingbird Books, 1975.

Myers, Edward. *When Parents Die: A Guide for Adults.* New York: Viking Penguin, 1986.

Niles, D. T. *As Seeing the Invisible.* New York: Harper & Brothers, 1961.

Nouwen, Henri J. M. *A Letter of Consolation.* San Francisco: Harper & Row, 1982.

Oates, Wayne E. *Pastoral Care and Counseling in Grief and Separation.* Philadelphia: Fortress Press, 1976.

Osterweis, Marian, and Fredrick Solomon, eds. *Bereavement: Reactions, Consequences, and Care.* Washington, DC: National Academy Press, 1984.

Price, Eugenia. *Getting Through the Night: Finding Your Way Through Grief.* San Francisco: Harper Collins, 1991.

Quezada, Adolfo. *Goodbye, My Son, Hello.* St. Meinrad, IN: Abbey Press, 1985.

Rogness, Alvin N. *Appointment with Death.* Nashville, TN: Thomas Nelson, 1972.

Rouner, Leroy S. *The Long Way Home.* South Bend, IN: Langford Books, 1989.

Rupp, Joyce. *Praying Our Goodbyes.* Notre Dame, IN: Ave Maria Press, 1988.

Schatz, William H. *Healing a Father's Grief.* Redmond, WA: Medic Publishing Co., 1984.

Shedd, Charlie W. *Remember, I Love You: Martha's Story.* San Francisco: Harper Collins, 1990.

Springteen, Anne. *Handful of Thorns: Poems of Grief.* Valparaiso, IN: Orchard House, 1977.

Tatelbaum, Judy. *The Courage to Grieve.* New York: Harper & Row, 1980.

Thompson, Mervin E. *When Death Touches Your life: Practical Help in Preparing for Death.* Minneapolis: Prince of Peace Publishing, 1986.

Trobisch, Ingrid. *Learning to Walk Alone: Personal Reflections on a Time of Grief.* Ann Arbor, MI: Vine Books, 1985.

———. "The Price of Loving." *The Lutheran* (March 29, 1986): 12–14.

Wolterstorff, Nicholas. *Lament for a Son.* Grand Rapids, MI: William B. Eerdmans, 1987.